Celebrating
the Year of Mercy

CELEBRATING
THE YEAR OF MERCY

BEGINS ON
THE FEAST OF THE IMMACULATE CONCEPTION
(December 8, 2015)

CONCLUDES ON
THE SOLEMNITY OF CHRIST THE KING
(November 20, 2016)

Compiled By
The Guardian Angel Zacchaeus
and his earthly ward,
Francesco of the Blessed Trinity

LEONINE PUBLISHERS
PHOENIX, ARIZONA

Copyright © 2015 Francesco Catanio

Author's note: "The Guardian Angel Zacchaeus" is a pen name, but the events and stories in this little book are otherwise accurate and true.

All rights reserved. No part of this book may be reproduced or transmitted in any form or by any means, electronic or mechanical, including photocopying, recording, or by any information storage or retrieval system now existing or to be invented, without written permission from the respective copyright holder(s), except for the inclusion of brief quotations in a review.

Scripture texts in this work are taken from the *New American Bible*, revised edition, © 2010, 1991, 1986, 1970, Confraternity of Christian Doctrine, Washington, D.C., and are used by permission of the copyright owner. All Rights Reserved. No part of the *New American Bible* may be reproduced in any form without permission in writing from the copyright owner.

Published by Leonine Publishers LLC
Phoenix, Arizona
USA

ISBN-13: 978-1-942190-21-9
Library of Congress Control Number: 2015959391

Printed in the United States of America
10 9 8 7 6 5 4 3 2 1

Visit us online at www.leoninepublishers.com
For more information: info@leoninepublishers.com

We dedicate this little book to

The Blessed Mother
and
Ethan Gerhart
http://www.caringbridge.org

Contents

Preface xi
Introduction 1
We Are Created to be Saints 3
The Faith Journey of Francesco 5

PART I
Pathways to Sainthood

Francesco's Thoughts on Sainthood 12
Rules on Being a Saint 13
Abandon Oneself to God's Will 14
Always Remain in God's Presence 15
Always Say *Yes* to God 16
Venerate the Blessed Mother of God 17
Love Impartially and Unconditionally 18
Frequent the Holy Sacraments 19
Stay in a State of Prayer 20
Emulate the Spirituality of the Saints 21
Ruminate on Holy Scripture 23
Give Up Attachments to Created Things 24
Faith, Hope, and Love: The God-Given Virtues
    We Receive at Baptism 25

PART II
Francesco's Preparations for the Year of Mercy

Introduction 28
Francesco's Thoughts 29
Daily Instructions for the Year of Mercy 30
Francesco's Checklist for Celebrating the Year of Mercy. . 33
Elaboration of Francesco's Checklist 36

PART III
Consecration to the Sacred and Immaculate Hearts

Introduction 46
The Story of Saint Maximilian Kolbe 47
The Story of Saint Louis de Montfort. 48
Saint Louis de Montfort's Way of Total Consecration. . . 50
Total Consecration to Jesus 50
Act of Consecration to Jesus through Mary 52
The Tradition of "Holy Voluntary Slavery" 55
Francesco's Spiritual Journal for June 2014 58
Francesco's Summarization 80
The Many Titles and Devotions of the Blessed
 Virgin Mary. 81

Mary the Mother of God	82
The Blessed Virgin Mary	83
The Immaculate Conception	83
Our Lady of the Assumption	84
Mary Queen of Peace	84
Mary Queen of All Saints	85
Our Lady of the Miraculous Medal	85
Our Lady of Perpetual Help	86
Our Lady of Mount Carmel	87
Our Lady of the Snows	88
Our Lady of Sorrows	89
Our Lady of Knock	90
Our Lady of Guadalupe	91
Our Lady of Lourdes	92
Our Lady of Fatima	93
Intercession	94
History and Origin of the Holy Rosary	95
Where to Find the Holy Rosary Today	97
Keeping a Spiritual Journal	98
Francesco's Spiritual Journal: January to March 2013	100
A Conclave to Elect a New Pope	104
References	129

Francesco consecrated himself to
Our Lady of Guadalupe
on December 8, 2007.

Preface
(By Francesco)

Pope Francis was elected to succeed Peter the Apostle on March 13, 2013. His brother cardinal, seated next to him in the conclave, reminded him to "not forget the poor." Taking the name "Francesco" (after the beloved saint and "Little Poor Man," Saint Francis of Assisi) the pope proclaimed that the "shepherd must smell like the sheep."

Pope Francis shunned the trappings of the Vatican palace, rode the public bus to personally pay his Vatican hotel bill, and opted for a humble Ford Focus in place of a BMW staff car. No extravagant red shoes for Francesco. Was all this just mere gesture? The world would soon be asking questions.

Each pope inherits the primary duty to proclaim "The Great Commission," that is, the final instructions of Jesus before He ascended into heaven: *Go forth into the world and preach the good news to all creatures.* Popes, saints, and disciples throughout the ages have expressed by word of mouth, or in writing, this "Great Commission." Pope Francis continually announces it, both in word and action. He calls it the "Joy of the Gospel."

I, Francesco of the Blessed Trinity, am preparing to celebrate the "Joy of the Gospel" and the Year of Mercy with Pope Francis in the company of the Mother of Mercy, Our Blessed Mother. This little book is the story of my journey in preparation.

As a first step, I'm prayerfully reading: *Porta Fidei* (the Door of Faith), *Evangelii Gaudium* (the Joy of the Gospel), and *Misericordiae Vultus* (the Bull of the Extraordinary Jubilee of Mercy).

Introduction

(By Me, Zacchaeus)

I am the Guardian Angel Zacchaeus, but that's not my real name. I officially became Francesco's guardian on December 26, 1947, when he took his first unassisted breath, but Francesco's not his real name. I call him "Francesco" because he has come to have a loving devotion to Saint Francis of Assisi. One of Francesco's pastors, Father Joe, a former Vietnamese Air Force pilot, suggested to his flock that everyone be mindful of their guardian angels, calling them lovingly by name. After taking Father Joe's advice to heart, Francesco gave me the nickname "Zacchaeus." He's especially fond of the short-in-stature tax collector who climbed a tree to see Jesus. I have overlooked this small indiscretion of Francesco's in taking liberties to "name" me, a High Order of creature. His love compels me to embrace his childlike innocence within my heart.

Francesco and I have been together now for over sixty-eight years. His wife of forty-five years is Bernadette, but that's not her real name. I gave her this nickname because Our Lady of Lourdes interceded to restore her lost eyesight in 1976.

It was no surprise to me when Francesco decided to totally consecrate himself to Jesus, through Our Blessed Mother. As a small boy he often played in his grandfather's woodworking shop, absorbed in his grandfather's stories about the Blessed Virgin Mary. I'm only surprised that it took Francesco so long to be consecrated.

Francesco's natural mother prayed the holy rosary almost every day, and she taught Francesco to pray it as well. In this little book I share Francesco's faith journey, his spirituality, and his life-long efforts to be in union with God's will. I call him "Francesco of the Blessed Trinity" because he's always trying to find ways to see the Holy Trinity in all things.

We Are Created to be Saints

Every human being, whether in the past, present, or future, is meant to be a saint. This was God's will when He created man and it forever remains His will. God, who is all goodness, created human beings in His own likeness, to be good. God placed into humanity a loving "monkey wrench": His magnanimous gift of free will. The good news is this: by abandoning himself to God's will, man chooses total union with God. However, the grim alternative is that women and men are free to love sin.

An early disciple once asked Jesus, "Teacher, how can I enter into eternal life?" The Lord replied, "You shall love God with your whole heart, your whole mind, and with all your strength, and love your neighbor as yourself." The choice to love or not to love is always up to the individual human being.

Regarding sainthood: it doesn't matter whether humans are idiot savants or scientific geniuses. The playing field is always level. As Saint Francis de Sales put it, "To be a saint is to be who you are and to be that well."

Francesco's spirituality begins with "Love." He surmised that God is "Love" and that if he lived in God's love, God would live in him. He accepted that God's greatest command was to love. Love God first, love self, and love all others. Following the teachings of Saint Ignatius, Francesco believes that God is in all things, and he agrees that creation is God's great gift, enabling all mankind to achieve a loving union with God.

The story of Francesco is an example of how all human beings can navigate a journey to sainthood. Despite being beset with temptations, human weakness, and the difficult challenge of surrendering free will, all human beings are created to be saints.

The Faith Journey of Francesco

Like the decades of the most holy rosary, Francesco has had joyous, luminous, sorrowful, and glorious times. He was born at Saint Joseph's Hospital, in Stockton, California, on December 26, 1947. Soon thereafter he resided in a government housing project called Sierra Vista. His father was a farm laborer and his mother stayed home with six sons. The age of reason begins Francesco's first living rosary decade.

Attending catechism classes in a neighbor's garage (using the Baltimore Catechism) is Francesco's earliest recollection of faith. His most lasting childhood memory on the purpose of his existence is "to know, love, and serve God." In Francesco's adolescent mind, this translated into becoming an altar server. He's served Mass for over fifty-five years now, most joyously at various daily Mass communities, wherever he's lived and traveled.

Francesco's family was very poor for quite some time, until his father got a chance to go to butcher's school. At one point there was a big flood and their government housing project was suddenly deluged. Francesco's family moved in with paternal grandparents, in what was then Stockton's juvenile gangland district. Right smack in the middle of gang wars, knifings, and shootings, his Knights of Columbus father founded a youth baseball league. Francesco's brother Michael so excelled in sports that an elite North Stockton high school, Saint Mary's High, wanted to recruit him for their basketball program. His brother made the all-city basketball team, earning scholarships for himself and all his brothers.

Francesco graduated from Saint Mary's High in 1966. The second decade of Francesco's living rosary is from about age eleven to twenty-one. The Blessed Mother interjected herself very early into his life by means of several spiritual role models.

Francesco's first spiritual role model (during his junior high school years) was a cousin who is now Mother Elizabeth of the Trinity, a Carmelite nun.

It seemed very puzzling to Francesco that this young, highly-pursued, strikingly beautiful high school cheerleader would desire to enter into the cloistered life. While Sister Elizabeth was in her novitiate, Francesco volunteered for service in the Vietnam War. The letters Sister Elizabeth sent to Francesco (which he frequently re-reads) are one of his few great treasures. In her spiritual correspondence, Sister Elizabeth introduced Francesco to "The Little Flower," Saint Therese; to Saint Teresa of Avila's book *The Interior Castle*; to Saint John of the Cross; and to Saint Francis de Sales. He would pray the Our Father, slowly and deliberately, each time he took off on a combat mission. Francesco had one hundred and twenty-four combat missions over Laos and Cambodia, and was decorated with the Bronze Star, three Air Medals, three Meritorious Service Medals, three Commendation Medals, the Vietnam Campaign and Service Medal, and the Vietnam Gallantry Cross with fourteen battle stars. I believe the Lord allowed him to win war decorations, in sequences of three, to keep him mindful of the Blessed Trinity.

The third decade of Francesco's living rosary is from about age twenty-two to thirty-two. He entered into the Sacrament of Holy Matrimony with a Thailand rice farmer's daughter, who had "escaped to the big city" to become a seamstress. Bernadette's father was one of the holiest people Francesco would ever encounter. Without neglecting his family or his rice crop, he was in the temple day and night. After listening to Francesco's story about the Catholic faith, he agreed to let him marry his daughter.

Francesco and his bride were married three times (another sign of the Blessed Trinity): in a Buddhist ceremony, at a Catholic Mass, and finally by a Justice of the Peace, to satisfy Thai law. They had three children: Calvin, Stephen, and Sarah. Francesco sheepishly named his first born, Calvin, after a boyhood friend. Calvin's baptismal name is Joseph.

The fourth decade of Francesco's living rosary is from the ages of thirty-three to forty-three. He and Bernadette attended Cursillo weekends and had "born again" experiences at around the same time. This period of time corresponds to the second half of Francesco's Air Force career, when he was an Intelligence Operations Specialist.

Residing at Myrtle Beach Air Force Base, then was the next of Francesco's spiritual role models: a local deacon and his wife Doris. Deacon Ed was a Chief Master Sergeant and the leader of the local Cursillo community. He sponsored Francesco's Cursillo weekend and also introduced him to the Liturgy of the Hours. He encouraged Francesco to join the Knights of Columbus. Francesco was overjoyed to attend Ed's funeral, many years later, where many people in Pennsylvania celebrated the holy deacon for the saint that he was.

Doris is alive and well, now living in Goldsboro, North Carolina, eighty-five years young, and still has Cursillo community group prayer meetings, remaining ever joyful in the Faith.

Francesco was next sent to Spain, where he was assigned to the USAFE Tactics School as Intelligence Librarian. This tactics school was Europe's equivalent to the "Top Gun" school depicted in the Tom Cruise movie. Francesco's three years in Spain brought him and his wife into intimate contact with the Blessed Virgin Mary.

One unexpected morning, Bernadette woke up unable to see, stricken with Macular Degeneration. Doctors in Spain and Germany, and two of the best military hospital facilities in Europe, were at a loss as to how they could be of any help.

A few weeks after the diagnosis, Francesco and Bernadette went on a pilgrimage to Lourdes. At their hotel, that first night, Jesus appeared to Francesco's wife in a dream, and told Bernadette to stop trying to worship Buddha and Him at the same time. He told her that she would be given back her sight after seven days. Back home, after leaving Lourdes, and on the seventh day, Bernadette could see as clearly as before. But there was a second miracle: she now had the capability to read English and the Holy Bible effortlessly. Her previous lack of English language proficiency had been a roadblock to studying the Faith.

Francesco's fifth decade was from about age forty-four to fifty-four. The highlight of his life was to consecrate himself to Our Lady of Guadalupe on December 8, 2007. He found himself part of a small group of twenty-two men and women on a guided pilgrimage, who were in the beginning all strangers except his friend of many years, John and his sister Mary. Francesco delighted in serving Mass each day for the priest in charge of their delegation. One of Francesco's fellow pilgrims had been diagnosed with prostate cancer and another had recently lost her husband to suicide. Francesco's brief correspondence with two fellow pilgrims helped lift their spirits.

In Francesco's living rosary, the fifth decade and beyond, he and Bernadette had cancer at the same time. Francesco had prostate cancer and Bernadette had breast cancer. God's grace flowed abundantly throughout those challenging times.

Bernadette was comforted in her mastectomy by having a Thai exchange doctor perform the surgery. This doctor was a woman young enough to be their daughter, and she lovingly treated Bernadette and Francesco as though they were her parents.

When Francesco was diagnosed with prostate cancer, the doctor said it was at such an aggressive stage that he had no more than five years to live. On the day that he showed up for his first radiation treatment, a woman Francesco knew from daily Mass at the hospital chapel turned out to be the cancer clinic receptionist. She assured Francesco that his cancer would be in the hands of the Blessed Virgin. She insisted that Francesco come to dinner at her house that evening.

When Francesco arrived for dinner, there were about fifty people praying the rosary for him. After the rosary had concluded, they all laid hands on Francesco, prayed over him, and left. The dinner that followed was with the receptionist, her mother-in-law, and the head radiologist from the cancer clinic. The doctor explained all the upcoming treatments for Francesco over a delightful dinner. Francesco would receive a protocol of forty-five radiation sessions and two years of hormonal injections.

Francesco and Bernadette visited their hometown funeral parlor, just in case, to make final arrangements for themselves. The funeral parlor lady cried throughout the whole visit. But there was no need for tears.

Francesco and Bernadette have been cancer-free now for many years, and are retired from two careers: Francesco had been a Chief Master Sergeant in the Air Force for twenty-three years and a juvenile hall counselor for fifteen years. They're thankful for and enjoy their two generous pensions and social security checks.

The spirituality of Francesco has evolved from a simple, childlike Baltimore Catechism lesson on how to "know, love, and serve God" to a much more complicated journey in faith. I know that Francesco's goal is to come full circle and return to a more childlike love of our Lord and His Blessed Mother.

One ever-present feature of Francesco's spirituality has been his fondness for sets of "three's." Francesco thinks in three's in order to contemplate the Blessed Trinity. I would describe Francesco's three-fold spirituality as Franciscan, Salesian, and Ignatian. He's taken a vow of poverty, embraces Saint Francis de

Sales' notion of "being who you are and being that well," and he strives to see God in all things.

Francesco's present identity is that of belonging entirely to Jesus by way of total consecration to the Immaculate Heart of His Blessed Mother Mary. In responding to the Blessed Virgin's example and her various requests, Francesco yearns to spend a great deal of the rest of his life pondering, praying, and doing penance, after her example. It is my delight to continue on as Francesco's guardian angel for more decades of his life.

I'm happy to invite you to join me as I record this latest episode in the spiritual journey of Francesco. I present it in three parts, naturally.

PART I

PATHWAYS TO SAINTHOOD

(Rules and Behaviors Common to All Saints)

Francesco's Thoughts on Sainthood

Becoming and remaining a "saint" is truly a life-long process. Some manage to achieve holiness at early stages of life (like Saint Anthony of Padua), while others begin their road to sainthood much later. It all starts with God's gift of faith. We then cherish God's gift of hope, and gradually come to embrace His gift of love. We will most likely sin every day of our reasoned lives, but freedom from sin is forever possible. After all, there are times when people have been sin-free for at least a minute, for as much as an hour, or even for an entire day. We must have been pleasing to God, in various behaviors, at one time or another.

By reading Holy Scripture, and probing into the lives of the Lord's early disciples, it's revealed that they were far from perfect. Jesus didn't come to call saints. As a matter of fact, He came to call sinners. We acknowledge first that we are sinners, then try our best to strive for sainthood.

A list of canonized saints would include the widest variety of men and women, but canonization is not the definitive measure of sanctity. There must be countless saints who are known to God and God alone.

One human being, however, totally abandoned herself to God's will from the very first moment of her existence. She was full of God's grace at conception, and God found special favor with her. By getting to know the Blessed Virgin Mary, we can learn how to love God with our whole being. No human being is a greater role model for how to love God than God's own mother.

In my personal thoughts about sainthood, many famous and some totally unknown saints have become my inspirations.

If you're already a saint, I hope the following writings may amuse you. If you are firmly on the road to sainthood, I hope they don't distract you. But should they encourage you, in some small way, I thank God for another of His many blessings.

Rules on Being a Saint
(Ten Behaviors Common to All Saints)

1. Abandon oneself to God's will.

2. Always remain in God's presence.

3. Always say *yes* to God.

4. Venerate the Blessed Mother of God.

5. Love impartially and unconditionally.

6. Frequent the sacraments.

7. Stay in a state of prayerfulness.

8. Emulate the spirituality of the saints.

9. Ruminate on Holy Scripture.
(Ruminate: to reflect upon, slowly and deeply, over and over again; from the Latin word ruminari, *"to chew the cud")*

10. Give up attachments to created things.

Abandon Oneself to God's Will

Abandonment to God's will means to surrender each moment of our life to God just as we are. We must surrender to God all that we think, say, and do. This is our simple recipe for sainthood. Should we master this, all manner of holy results will follow.

The Lord Jesus Christ is a divine being who truly became man. This enables us to be imitators of God's Son, who is both human and divine. Jesus is our key to discerning and doing God's will. We strive to learn everything possible about ourselves and all there is to know about Jesus. We take care that our endeavors are fully in union with God's will, just as Jesus always did the will of His Father: "Thy kingdom come, Thy will be done, on earth as it is in heaven."

Human beings cannot know the mind of God, and our human descriptions of God are simply inadequate. But God communicates with us through our understanding, and we know that God is something eternally different from us.

We approach the apprehension of God's will by accepting, in faith, that our free will comes from Him as a loving gift. From the moment we reach the age of reason, up to the hour of our death, we make our own choices. God's gift of free will sets us apart from all other earthly creatures. Regardless of how we choose to exercise our free will, it can never be given back. It is a perplexing thing. It permits us to obey or disobey God, to seemingly please or displease Him, whenever we like.

How can we discern God's will and know what pleases Him? We heed the advice of Our Blessed Mother who said at the wedding feast of Cana, "Do whatever He tells you to do." We must trust Jesus and endeavor to be ourselves, trying our best to do that well.

Always Remain in God's Presence

We must take control of time and frequently be with God in silence. A song entitled "You are Mine," with lyrics by David Haas, has God saying: "I will come to you in the silence. I will lift you from all your fears. You will hear My voice. I claim you as My choice. Be still and know I am here…Do not be afraid, I am with you. I have called you each by name. Come and follow Me. I will bring you home. I love you and you are Mine." God is forever present to us when we are still and present to Him.

Psalm 139:1–7

Lord, you have probed me, you know me:
you know when I sit and stand;
you understand my thoughts from afar.
You sift through my travels and my rest;
with all my ways you are familiar.
Even before a word is on my tongue,
Lord, you know it all.
Behind and before you encircle me,
and rest your hand upon me.
Such knowledge is too wonderful for me,
far too lofty for me to reach.
Where can I go from your spirit?
From your presence, where can I flee?

There are so many opportunities, in our busy lives, to enjoy God's presence. Sitting in the dentist or barber's chair provides an opportunity, as does being stuck in traffic. If we open our hearts, and invite God to pay us a visit, He comes to us in the silence. In the tranquil silence, God is overflowing with love.

Always Say Yes to God

When fleeting good thoughts enter our minds, they can be inspirations from our Heavenly Father. We can always say *yes* to God.

Whenever crucial decisions come, we turn to prayer. If we're struggling to find a clear solution, maybe it's better to do nothing. We trust God to control all circumstances. Yes, He's truly with us, even as we are formed in our mothers' wombs. God forever knows our innermost thoughts and desires. In times of uncertainty we must stay patient and allow God to be God.

Communications from God are rarely clear or momentous (like Saint Peter being told in a dream to go to the house of Simon the Tanner). More likely they will come as very faint encouragements. "Tune into something else," God may suggest, while we're surfing the Internet.

God's guardian angels, are constant protectors at our side. If we should inadvertently take a wrong exit while driving, enjoy the detour. It may very well be an act of mercy from God, as He helps us avoid some unforeseen danger.

We sometimes hear voices in our minds, independent of our own intellects. *We are not crazy!* This is just our conscience, debating right from wrong. Of course God is on the "right" side of the argument. The more we remain in God's company, the more we will readily recognize the right.

The more we open our hearts to God's inspirations, the more we hear His voice. When we make prayer a daily routine, we sometimes learn about actions that we should pursue. When these inclinations seem good in themselves, don't be afraid. Always say *yes!* Trustingly respond to God's will.

Venerate the Blessed Mother of God

Those outside the Catholic Church have sometimes objected to what they think is "adoration" of the Blessed Virgin Mary. Christians and non-Christians alike have often made this claim. However, there's a huge difference between veneration and adoration. Mary is just a human being: but she happens to be the greatest human being of all.

Mary has a special honor in history because she is the Mother of God. The Mother of God is infinitely pleasing to Him. Before she was conceived in her mother's womb, God already had plans for her to be the Mother of Jesus, our Lord. Gabriel, the Angel of God, pronounced: "Hail full of grace, the Lord is with you!"

Our Blessed Mother stood at the foot of the cross with the disciple John, while Jesus in His dying breath said, "Woman, behold your son," and to His beloved disciple He said, "Behold your Mother." This is when Our Lady officially became the spiritual mother of the Church.

Popes and saints throughout the centuries have written volumes on how they personally were devoted to the Blessed Virgin Mary, and have recommended consecration to her as the best pathway to a saintly life.

We can come to know the Mother of God by reading everything we can about her. Our Lady has well over five hundred honors and titles, many of which are from visitations she's made throughout the life of the Church. Three most notable titles are "Our Lady of Guadalupe," "Our Lady of Fatima," and "Our Lady of Lourdes." What wonderful apparitions these were!

Love Impartially and Unconditionally

Perhaps it is an easier challenge to love God, who we cannot see, while our most difficult challenge is to love our neighbors, family, and friends, who we constantly see.

Some of the earliest known Scripture was written in ancient Greek. But unlike modern-day English, the Greeks had three distinct words for "love." "Eros," which is an erotic and sensual love; "Philia," which is a brotherly love; and "Agape," an impartial, unconditional, and self-sacrificing love. "Agape" is the love Jesus is talking about when He says, "Love the Lord your God with all your heart," "Love your neighbor as yourself," and "Love your enemy."

The Bible has more than seven hundred references to the word "love." So it's plain to see that Christianity is all about love. The Gospel of Saint John says, "God is love, and he who lives in love, lives in God, and God in him." God had so much love for us that He sent His only Son to die for our sins, so that we might have eternal life.

In the first book of Corinthians, chapter thirteen describes love in a very impartial and unconditional way:

> If I speak in human and angelic tongues, but do not have love, I am a resounding gong or a clashing symbol. And if I have the gift of prophecy and…have faith so as to move mountains, but do not have love, I am nothing.

If I give away everything I own…but do not have love, I gain nothing. Love is patient, love is kind. It is not jealous, [love] is not pompous, it is not inflated, it is not rude, it does not seek its own interests…[Love] bears all things, believes all things, hopes all things, endures all things. Love never fails.

Frequent the Holy Sacraments

Jesus gave us seven sacraments. The first is Baptism. The Holy Eucharist (Holy Communion) was instituted at the Last Supper. The other five sacraments are Confirmation (the gift of the Holy Spirit, by the laying on of hands), Reconciliation (confession and the forgiveness of sins), Holy Orders (the ordination of bishops, priests, and deacons), Holy Matrimony (the spiritual union of a man and woman), and lastly, Anointing of the Sick. Jesus established all these sacraments as a means to provide God's grace.

The Holy Eucharist is "the source and summit of the Christian life." The Body and Blood, Soul and Divinity of Jesus, is truly present in the Holy Eucharist. When Jesus first revealed this to His disciples, many of them refused to accept it, and returned to their former ways of life. It's still a stumbling block for many today. But as Jesus said, "If you do not eat my flesh and drink my blood, you will not have life within you." Those of us who believe are grateful for the gift of faith.

To receive Confirmation is to gain the grace and courage to proclaim the Good News. Christ will give to each of us the amount of grace we need.

Jesus said to Peter and His other apostles, "Whose sins you forgive are forgiven." This was a delegation of authority. It is God alone who forgives sins, while priests and bishops are instruments of His grace. Through their consecration, they fulfill the urgent need of reassurance that our sins are truly forgiven.

Today we can experience the Sacrament of the Anointing of the Sick much more frequently than in the past, where it was usually administered to those on their deathbed. Many parishes now offer this sacrament on a weekly basis, as part of Saturday Mass.

Both the Sacrament of Holy Orders and the Sacrament of Holy Matrimony are unique in that the persons involved are the instruments of God's grace. The mindset of all deacons, priests, bishops, and married couples should be, "How can we be constant channels of God's grace?"

Stay in a State of Prayer

"God come to my assistance, Lord make haste to help me." "Heavenly Father, please hear our prayer." It's important that we ask God to hear us whenever we lift up our hearts in prayer.

We take time in the morning to greet the Holy Mother of God and our guardian angels. We remember to say grace before meals: "Bless us, O Lord, and these Thy gifts, which we are about to receive from Thy bounty, through Christ our Lord, Amen." Saint Paul said to pray always. It's not as impossible as it may sound. The secret is to employ naturally appropriate prayers at the right time. It's advisable to venture "outside the box" sometimes. When driving our cars we might pray for pedestrians we observe on the sidewalks. "Lord, bless and protect them and fill them with Your love and Your grace." Simple short prayers can help fill our days with joy. A holy Irish priest once taught his parishioners to employ four categories of prayer: Adoration,

Contrition, Thanksgiving, and Supplication. The first letters of these words form the acronym "A.C.T.S." ("S" can also stand for "Surrender.")

It's God we first encounter as we begin each new day of our lives. This first waking hour is a very good time for "A.C.T.S." "Adoration": reflect on the fact that God is God and we are not. In the blink of an eye we would cease to exist if God so desired. Yet here we are, full of life, ready to experience a new day. We offer to God, for His greater glory, all we are about to think, say, and do. Through "Contrition," we recall the times we've been displeasing to God. In "Thanksgiving," we express to God our gratitude for the many blessings we now enjoy. Finally, we ask God for whatever our hearts desire. Knock and the door will be opened. Ask and you will receive.

The last hour before we sleep is a good time to examine our activities of the day. Have we been pleasing to God? What can we do to improve? Words are not always necessary in prayer. Our loving God knows our innermost desires and how we love Him. Pray silently and God will often give you direction and inspiration.

Emulate the Spirituality of the Saints

Saint Francis de Sales (1567–1622) wrote a spiritual guide for ordinary men and women called "Introduction to the Devout Life." At that time, "holiness" was thought to be only for priests, nuns, and monks. Saint Francis changed all that by giving spiritual direction to lay people in their ordinary lives. He taught that "we are all created to be saints, and the formula for sainthood is to be who we are, and to be that well."

There are so many canonized saints to choose from for spiritual insights. A good way to accomplish this is to get a Catholic parish calendar and look up the biographies of the saints as their feast days appear throughout the liturgical year.

There is a great variety of saints, all of them ordinary people who led extraordinary spiritual lives: popes, kings, former knights like Saint Francis of Assisi, and an obscure Carmelite nun named Thérèse of Lisieux. Internet videos provide wonderful short biographies on the saints.

Emulating saints does not necessarily mean copying them. For example, Saint Maximilian Kolbe found himself in a Nazi concentration camp. One day the commandant was about to execute nine men as an example to the inmates, after one of them had escaped the camp. Father Kolbe decided to substitute his own life for that of a man with a wife and children. Saint Maximilian Kolbe is also famous for his devotion to the Blessed Virgin Mary, and his formula for consecrating one's life to her Immaculate Heart. Although we might not have the opportunity to give up our lives for someone, we can imitate his selflessness and his love for Our Lady. Our personal spirituality, moderate or heroic, will never be out of our reach.

In honoring the lives of the saints, we might remember our own family members, never canonized perhaps, but very possibly saints, nonetheless.

Ruminate on Holy Scripture

The word "ruminate" means to reflect slowly and deeply on a particular matter. (It comes from the Latin word *ruminari*, "to chew the cud.") This is a good approach to take when praying and studying Holy Scripture.

We accept in faith that Holy Scripture, made up of the Old and New Testaments, although written by men, is inspired by the Holy Spirit. This wonderful "library" of books (forty-six in the Old Testament and twenty-seven in the New Testament) is the love story of God and man.

When we study and pray over Scripture, we may sometimes take the words of Jesus for granted. They may become overly familiar, sometimes even stale and empty. People in Nazareth, Jesus' hometown, reacted to our Lord's words by trying to throw Him off a cliff. The people of Capernaum, on the other hand, were astounded by His teachings, because He taught with authority and not like the scribes.

There is an ancient method of scriptural study, called "Lectio Divina," which is Latin for "Divine Reading." It may be the best method for "chewing the cud" over God's Word. Lectio Divina uses a four-step process of reading, meditation, prayer, and contemplation of Scripture, all to promote and enhance communion with God. First, a passage of Scripture is read; then the meaning is reflected upon; and lastly, reflection is followed by prayer and contemplation. A detailed description of the "Lectio Divina" method can readily be found on the Internet. Cardinal Archbishop Thomas Collins of Toronto has some wonderful sessions of Lectio Divina that can be found in Internet videos.

Give Up Attachments to Created Things

The world is full of the Lord's goodness! We already know that God owns everything, with just one exception: His loving gift of free will. In the Book of Genesis, God tells us to take stewardship over all the earth. So if everything on the earth is entrusted to us, how can we have no attachment to created things? The key word in regard to worldly things is "attachment."

One day, as Jesus walked along, a rich man approached and asked Him how he could get to heaven. Jesus replied, "Keep the commandments." And the rich young man said, "I've done so since my youth." "One more thing," Jesus added, "sell everything you own, give the money to the poor, then come and follow Me." The young man went away sad, since he loved and possessed so many things. How can we ever go through the eye of a needle if we remain camels? How do we rid ourselves of earthly attachments? The solution is "holy indifference."

The Acts of the Apostles tells how Saint Paul embraced holy indifference. Perhaps if Saint Paul were alive today, he'd declare, "I'm content when I'm served a can of Campbell's soup, and happy to have *soup du jour* at the finest French restaurant."

Having no attachment to created things doesn't quite match our personal fondness for movies, ice cream, batter-fried jumbo shrimp, peanut butter, slot machines, baseball, and more. We really like these things, and indulge in them on a regular basis. However, when we exercise the concept of "holy indifference" it is a very good thing. If shrimp suddenly becomes extinct then we won't really mind.

Faith, Hope, and Love: The God-Given Virtues We Receive at Baptism

(Francesco's thoughts)

God made us and we belong to Him. He has showered us with many gifts. He's humbled Himself to share in our humanity, and He promises us the ultimate gift of eternal life. We accept God's gifts of faith, hope, and love and go forward on our lifelong journey in the quest to be saints.

Jesus told Nicodemus that he would not attain eternal life (sanctity) unless he was born again of the Holy Spirit. This takes place at the moment we accept the gift of faith. The Centurion, through his humility, and his whole household as well, were filled with the Holy Spirit. "Amazing grace, how sweet the sound...the hour I first believed."

Hope in our future eternal union with God is only acquired from His grace as well. Once we accept God's gift of faith, hope will naturally follow. Then comes love! It would be utterly impossible for us to love if we were simple ordinary creatures. To our amazement, God has created us with immortal souls, enabling us to have "agape" love.

God (who we can't actually see) is faintly visible in the things we see on earth. We have many reminders of the Blessed Trinity in God's creation. Earth, wind, and fire; breakfast, lunch, and dinner; the trimesters of pregnancy; animals, vegetables, and minerals; just to name a few. God has left His indelible footprints.

We humans are known to hurt one another even after long-shared love. It's not easy to love people. Jesus was asked, "How many times must I forgive my brother?" "Seven times seventy times," He replied, since this was a metaphor for "always." Loving is never easy because people have unique love needs. We need only to fill our quivers full of Christ's love, then take all the shots needed to break all barriers. "How many times must I love my brother?" Seven times seventy times! *Always!*

PART II

FRANCESCO'S PREPARATIONS FOR THE YEAR OF MERCY

Introduction
(By Me, Zacchaeus)

Francesco has been pondering the idea that the upcoming Year of Mercy actually began three years ago, when Pope Benedict XVI declared a "Year of Faith." The Pope said the Year of Faith would begin October 11, 2012 (the fiftieth anniversary of the opening of the Second Vatican Council) and conclude November 24, 2013 (the Feast of Christ the King). On the concluding day of Pope Benedict's "Year of Faith," the newly-elected Pope Francis issued the apostolic exhortation *Evangelii Gaudium* (the Joy of the Gospel).

To Francesco there seems to have arrived a time of cleansing and renewal throughout the Church: beginning with Pope Francis' election, on March 13, 2013, until exactly two years passed, when he announced a Year of Mercy on March 13, 2015. Francesco supposes that this time period coincides with the three-year period during which Our Lord first proclaimed His Good News of the Gospel. With the Feast of Pentecost approaching at the time of this announcement, many have come to believe that the Holy Spirit is calling for a renewal of "The Great Commission" in our time.

In the third year of his pontificate, Pope Francis has declared a "Year of Mercy." Francesco, overwhelmed with joy and excitement, recalls the first words of the "Salve Regina": "Hail, Holy Queen, Mother of Mercy!" Something wonderful is always happening in the Church.

Francesco's Thoughts

The Lenten season and Easter observances of 2015 have allowed me to reach a fresh new level in my consecration to the Blessed Mother. Many blessings in prayer, study, and action have cascaded upon me, and given me new insight into my purpose.

The election of Pope Francis, a Jesuit priest, led me to participate in a thirty-four-week online Ignatian retreat sponsored by Creighton University. The retreat started its first week September 14–20, 2014, and week thirty-four concluded May 3–9, 2015, in alignment with the liturgical calendar. It was a wonderful spiritual journey. All those weeks served as spiritual background music for me amidst my everyday activities.

The online retreat was a catalyst for me to celebrate something special throughout the 2015 Lenten and Easter seasons. It resulted in a rich experience of fellowship and love among three communities I joined, and it climaxed during an Easter retreat in a very special place: Christ the King Retreat Center in Citrus Heights, Sacramento, California.

My first Lenten season visit was to the Missionaries of Christ Crucified. They are a religious order of lay brothers and sisters who advance the teaching of Luisa Picaretta, "The Little Daughter of the Divine Will."

The second community was the Women's Prayer and Scripture Study Group of Holy Rosary Parish in Woodland, California. In this group, twenty-four holy women gather to pray and study Scripture each week.

The third and final community visited was Our Mother of Good Counsel, Legion of Mary Presidium, at Saint Mary's Parish in Vacaville, California.

The fresh new level in my consecration to the Blessed Mother is that I have become a member of the Legion of Mary. After reading the life story of the founder, Venerable Frank Duff, his treatise on sainthood, and his Legion of Mary manual, I joyfully discerned that the Legion of Mary was a wonderful spiritual framework in which to celebrate the Year of Mercy.

I've formed my Year of Mercy preparations knowing that everything I may come up with is to be "background music," always deferring to the guidance of Our Blessed Mother one day at a time. I seem to busy myself planning and organizing spiritual activities without realizing that the paths I choose may well be set aside by the Blessed Mother. I am content with that. I am all hers, and am happy to have her do with me whatever she wishes. I must remain focused on my first inclination: to celebrate the Year of Mercy in adoration of the Blessed Trinity. I hope to begin each day with the following daily instructions:

Daily Instructions for the Year of Mercy

My first priority is to reserve the first waking hour of each day to entering into God's presence. I will fully adore God and humbly assess my nothingness while discerning whether I am in a state of grace. Should my evaluation result in a feeling that I am not in a state of grace, I will do nothing else until receiving absolution. If grace is what I discern, I will remain in contemplation of God's majesty until reaching an appropriate moment to begin my morning offering. My morning offering will be evaluated for clarity and simplicity from time to time. I will structure my morning offering in a way that is reminiscent of the Blessed Trinity. The intended recipients of the morning offering are Jesus, Mary, and Joseph. It will conclude with a renewal of consecration to the Blessed Mother. My second priority is to fully participate in the Holy Sacrifice of the Mass so as to worthily receive the Holy Eucharist. In concert with receiving Holy Communion, the Word of God in Holy Scripture must be daily received in prayerful study.

My third priority is to fulfill already-known requests from the Blessed Mother. This certainly includes a daily rosary for penance, as she requested when appearing at Fatima. I must remember my Legion of Mary obligations. I will recall the wedding at Cana and the Mother of God's first entreaty: "Do whatever He tells you to do." (Whenever in doubt, consult the Blessed Mother, who is always perfectly conformed to the Divine Will.) I will collect, day after day, whatever standing entreaties the Blessed Mother may impart.

Once the first, second, and third priorities are fulfilled: I am free to engage in my usual occupations. It would be well to infuse prayer, study, and apostolic action in all occupations. Before starting any action, I will invoke God's blessing, so that my actions may reflect God's divine will. I should focus entirely on any person who enters into my life, as if Jesus Himself were engaging me. I will enter into God's presence at day's end to examine my conscience. Once I discern what may have been pleasing or displeasing to God, I will silently contemplate God's majesty until the moment arrives to rest until my next first waking hour.

Morning Offering

Jesus, I desire to live in Your Sacred Heart, and perfectly conform to the Blessed Trinity's divine will, one day at a time. Consecrate me to the Immaculate Heart of Your Blessed Mother, and allow me to surrender my obedience through her. Jesus, Mary, and Joseph, pray for me.

Suscipe of Saint Ignatius

Take, Lord, and receive all my liberty, my memory, my understanding, and my entire will, all I have and call my own. You have given all to me. To you, Lord, I return it. Everything is yours; do with it what you will. Give me only your love and your grace, that is enough for me.

Daily Consecration to the Immaculate Heart of Mary

Queen of all creation: I love you. I renew my consecration to you and your Immaculate Heart. Please accept me, my dear Mother, and do with me whatever you wish. Oh loving handmaid of the Lord, my life, my sweetness, and my hope. I am all yours.

Francesco's Checklist for Celebrating the Year of Mercy

1. Prayerfully listen to Frank Padilla's talk (to be found through EWTN) telling all about "The Great Commission."

Note: Remaining checklist items are composed in three parts to celebrate, in adoration of the Blessed Trinity, the Year of Mercy.

2. Prayerfully read these three documents:

    1) Year of Faith proclamation by Pope Benedict XVI
    2) Joy of the Gospel proclamation by Pope Francis
    3) Year of Mercy proclamation by Pope Francis

3. Organize the resources needed to celebrate the Year of Mercy for your:

    Private prayer
    Private study
    Personal apostolic action

4. Join three Catholic organizations for the Year of Mercy (perhaps more) to experience community-involved works of mercy.

The Corporal Works of Mercy

Feed the hungry
Give drink to the thirsty
Clothe the naked
Shelter the homeless
Visit the sick
Visit the imprisoned
Bury the dead

The Spiritual Works of Mercy

Admonish the sinner
Instruct the ignorant
Counsel the doubtful
Comfort the sorrowful
Bear wrongs patiently
Forgive all injuries
Pray for the living and the dead

5. With the liturgical calendar as a foundation, devise a system to schedule daily, weekly, and monthly Year of Mercy priorities and occupations along with the Pontifical Council's Year of Mercy agenda.

6. Schedule attendance at three spiritual retreats:

    Advent Season (Franciscan Retreat Center)
    Ordinary Time (Ignatian Retreat Center…online retreat permitted)
    Easter Triduum (Passionist Retreat Center)

7. Select three geographical counties within your diocese to which you've never been, and plan to attend Holy Mass at three parishes (nine parishes total) within each of their boundaries.

8. Begin rebuilding your spiritual library by acquiring three books per quarter for the Year of Mercy, so that one text is purchased prior to the start of each month to be read one per month for the span of the year.

9. With Father Dolindo's "Surrender Prayer" novena as your morning prayer novena of choice, select two other novenas (to comprise three novenas per quarter) in accordance with various feast days of the Blessed Mother, and other significant events on the liturgical calendar.

10. Renew enthronement of your home to the Sacred Heart of Jesus, and refresh your knowledge of the Sacred Heart and First Saturday devotions.

Elaboration of Francesco's Checklist
(By Me, Zacchaeus)

What Francesco is doing with his Blessed Trinity checklist is spreading a table of plenty for himself. He hopes to partake of it day by day, as though it were a wonderful buffet of choices: but always with the consent, and in the company of, his Blessed Mother.

Once his framework of bookmarked Internet resources, scheduled retreats, spiritual books on order, membership in apostolic groups, and other odds and ends are set in place, Francesco will begin each day of the Year of Mercy discerning God's will under the mantle of the Blessed Mother.

Francesco's wife Bernadette is fully onboard with him, celebrating the Year of Mercy. She's become an auxiliary member of the Legion of Mary and has been praying the Legion "Catena" every day with Francesco. Their kitchen table is becoming a holy place.

Francesco's plans to celebrate the Year of Mercy seem overly ambitious at first sight. So in the months following November 20, 2016, I hope to write a second little book to chronicle how well Francesco actually does throughout the Year of Mercy, and what adventures he actually encounters.

For any who desire to formulate their own plans for celebrating the Year of Mercy: feel free to use any and all of the suggestions in this little book. We understand that our journeys in faith are all very unique. I do, however, highly recommend consecration to Our Blessed Mother, in some form, before beginning your journey.

CHECKLIST ITEM 1.
(Prayerfully Listen to Frank Padilla's Talk "The Great Commission")

Frank Padilla is the servant general and founder of Couples for Christ (CFC). CFC's mission is to renew the family and defend life.

Frank is a member of the Pontifical Council for the Family. He made the decision to follow Christ in 1981 and has since then dedicated his life to serving Him. As of April 2010, Couples for Christ is doing its work in sixty-six countries with more than 120,000 members. Frank is married, has five children and five (going on six) grandchildren. He resides in Antipolo City in the Philippines.

Francesco selects Frank Padilla's talk on "The Great Commission" to begin his preparations for the Year of Mercy because he considers this short-yet-complete pronouncement by Frank to be the most simple and easy version of Christ's original commission. What Pope Francis has wonderfully and beautifully promulgated in his exhortation, *Evangelii Gaudium*, Frank Padilla has condensed into a talk that is only a few minutes long.

CHECKLIST ITEM 2.
(Prayerfully Read the Three Papal Documents: *Year of Faith*, *Joy of the Gospel*, and *Year of Mercy*)

These documents, the first by Pope Benedict XVI and the last two by Pope Francis, are invitations to renew a "life in Christ." Since they are addressed to the whole world, parts of them may not seem entirely relevant to the average American Catholic. No matter; sift through them like a gold miner panning for gold. When a beautiful nugget of gold is discovered, employ the prayerful reading method "Lectio Divina." The Year of Mercy proclamation by Pope Francis is rather manageable and can be easily digested in one sitting. This should be done. It's our invitation to fully participate in the Year of Mercy. As Pope Francis makes ready to symbolically open the doors of the Church, remember that we are the Church, who should make ready to open the "doors of our hearts" on December 8, 2015.

CHECKLIST ITEM 3.
(Organize Resources for Your Prayer, Study, and Apostolic Action)

Francesco takes a particular concept of daily prayer, study, and action from his experience in the Cursillo Community back in 1979. The concept of the three-legged stool representing prayer, study, and action is one of the marks of the Blessed Trinity, which Francesco so often delights in. The Internet has proven to be one of Francesco's most valuable resources to aid in prayer, foster his study habits, and to provide initiative and motivation for apostolic action.

Three specific websites have been part of Francesco's daily spiritual diet: the U.S. Catholic Bishops Daily Scripture site, the Creighton University Daily Reflection Calendar, and the Saint Louis University Sunday Worship site. Francesco regularly visits three online daily-televised Mass sites: The EWTN daily Mass, the Sydney Australia daily Mass, and the Toronto Canada daily Mass. Praise music is an essential component of Francesco's spirituality, and his favorite artists are the Saint Louis Jesuits and John Michael Talbot. He loves all forms of Marian hymns and litanies.

These resources for prayer and study provide ideas and inspirations for apostolic action. Francesco has been led to much apostolic action by simply listening to various homilies presented online by the Franciscan Friars of Our Lady of Guadalupe. Francesco has bookmarked a substantial library of Internet websites for ready access. He refers to it as his "Table of Plenty."

CHECKLIST ITEM 4.
(Join Three Catholic Organizations for the Year of Mercy)

Francesco has chosen the Legion of Mary; the Women's Wednesday Morning Scripture Study Group at Holy Rosary Parish in Woodland, California; and "Loaves and Fishes" of Sacramento, California, for the three apostolic communities through which to celebrate the "Year of Mercy."

Francesco listened to Internet videos telling the life stories of Legion of Mary founder Frank Duff and two other Venerables, Edel Quinn and Alfie Lamb. He soon located Frank Duff's manual on the Legion and the next morning, his brief treatise on becoming a saint. He telephoned the parish office at Saint Mary's Church in Vacaville and inquired about the Legion of Mary. The receptionist said, "Magee, the president of our legion, happens to be here right now; you can speak with her." Francesco knew that Magee's presence there that morning was a clear sign for him to join the Legion. His wife Bernadette joined as an auxiliary member, so that she and Francesco could pray the daily "Catena."

While Francesco was celebrating Lent in 2015, he happened to see an article in the Holy Rosary Parish bulletin, inviting anyone to come to a Bible study on Wednesday mornings. He went to a session on a whim and found the place full of the Holy Spirit. There were twenty-four wonderful women, and Francesco joined as the only man. Their study resource for Lent was the movie entitled "The Way." Easter came and went, and a second man, Michael, joined the group.

Francesco and Bernadette were searching for a place to share their involvement in raising funds for the poor throughout the Year of Mercy. Bernadette suggested "Mary's House," an organization run by the Sisters of Mercy in Sacramento, California, in association with the "Loaves and Fishes."

CHECKLIST ITEM 5.
(Schedule Your Year of Mercy Liturgical Calendar Activities)

Knowing that the Blessed Mother may lead him by a different path, Francesco has nonetheless previewed the Year of Mercy liturgical calendar and marked his attendance and various activity participations: week by week, month by month, and for the over-all year.

Checklist Item 6.
(Schedule Attendance at Three Spiritual Retreats)

Francesco has signed up for a three-day silent retreat at San Damiano Franciscan Retreat Center in Danville, California. He and Bernadette attended an Easter Triduum retreat there in the 1990s. He hopes to pray the twenty-four hours of the passion with Luisa Picaretta, the "Little Daughter of the Divine Will," to begin the celebration of the Year of Mercy. To satisfy his desire that his second retreat be a Jesuit one, he's decided to re-attend the thirty-four week online retreat with Creighton University. Francesco's third and final retreat during the Year of Mercy will be to join his wife, Bernadette, in an Easter retreat at Christ the King Passionist Retreat Center in Citrus Heights, California. Francesco hopes to put on a new mindset of mercy for his retreat attendance as well as for all other activities throughout the upcoming holy year.

Checklist Item 7.
(Attending Holy Mass in Various Diocesan Parishes)

Years ago, Francesco embarked on a journey to visit all of the California missions and all of the parishes in his Sacramento diocese. At the time, the number of parishes numbered fewer than one hundred. He was successful in visiting every mission, but visited only around fifty parishes. This coming Year of Mercy, Francesco would like to bring back the fond memories he had as an itinerant daily Mass attendee. He has earmarked three counties, three parishes in each, and nine total visits, hoping to use the opportunity to complete the First Friday Devotions.

Checklist Item 8.
(Begin rebuilding your spiritual library)

Francesco has selected classic spiritual books which he first encountered during his youth, and the writings of the popes who had served during his lifetime, as the primary selections for his "one book per month" for the Year of Mercy. He'll postpone actual selections until November of 2015.

Checklist Item 9.
(Selecting your novena prayers for the Year of Mercy)

Francesco was introduced to the Surrender Novena of Father Dolindo by the Marian Missionaries of Christ Crucified in Vacaville, California. He was attending their Tuesday morning "Divine Will Study Group." Francesco surmised that the Blessed Mother wanted him to pray this novena continually, so he has adopted it as part of his daily prayer routine. This particular novena Francesco offers exclusively to the Blessed Mother. With her permission, he offers other novenas for the intentions of family and friends and those he discovers to be in need of special prayers. He's selected all nine of his novenas for the Year of Mercy and has bookmarked his favorite versions. The Blessed Mother usually reveals who should be prayed for.

Checklist Item 10.
(Renew Sacred Heart Enthronement for Your Home)

Francesco had his home blessed and enthroned to the Sacred Heart of Jesus by Father Pablo Farfan, a Peruvian priest and pastor of his home parish on September 12, 2007. At the time, Francesco was making final preparations for his pilgrimage to Mexico City to consecrate himself to the Blessed Mother. Father Farfan has been assigned to many parishes since then and is no longer pastor of Saint Peter's. However, he happens to be living in nearby Vacaville and may be available to renew the blessing of Francesco's home. Francesco must consult his partner in holy matrimony, Bernadette, who is the hostess for such occasions.

PART III

CONSECRATION TO THE SACRED AND IMMACULATE HEARTS

(A Sure Pathway to Sainthood)

INTRODUCTION
(By Me, Zacchaeus)

Consecration to the Holy Mother of God goes way back. The first disciple to be so consecrated was probably Saint John (the apostle Jesus loved) at the foot of the cross. Over the next two thousand years or so, throughout the life of the Church, countless saints have followed Saint John's example. Some of the most famous consecrated disciples are Saint Maximilian Kolbe, Saint Louis de Montfort, Saint Pope John Paul II, and Blessed Mother Teresa of Calcutta, to name a few. Many thousands more have consecrated themselves to the Blessed Virgin Mary as well.

Holy Mother Church reminds us that we are all consecrated through Baptism, and set apart to exclusively serve God. Persons, places, and things can be consecrated. Church buildings are consecrated and set apart as places of worship. Chalices and patens, for example, are consecrated and set aside to receive the Sacred Body and Blood of Our Lord. It would be a desecration to use these places and things for any other purpose. Bishops, priests, deacons, and religious are consecrated and set aside for unique lives of service. We are all consecrated within God's creation: we are made in His own image.

Saint Maximilian Kolbe likened consecration to enlistment in an army under the command of Mary Immaculate. He called his congregation "The Militia of the Immaculata." Consecration to the Blessed Virgin Mary is being set apart for the express purpose of battling the forces of evil. Our Blessed Mother is the "Field Commanding General" and Jesus her Son is our "Commander in Chief." Until Jesus returns in His glory, the Holy Virgin Mary has full authority to lead the fight against darkness and evil. That's one way of looking at it.

The Story of Saint Maximilian Kolbe

(Compiled by Francesco)

Raymond Kolbe was born on January 8, 1894, in Poland. He felt drawn to follow the Lord and love the Virgin Mary, who offered him two crowns: one white (symbolizing purity) and the other red (symbolizing martyrdom). As a young boy, he joined the Franciscan Friars and received the religious name Maximilian. Shortly afterward, he was sent to Rome and completed studies in philosophy and theology. On October 16, 1917, he established a congregation called the "Militia of the Immaculata," a public association of the faithful, which is now active internationally. The Militia's spirituality consists of living a total consecration to Our Blessed Mother, in order to attain a more perfect union with Jesus, and to collaborate with her in spreading Christ's kingdom throughout the world. Ordained a priest in 1918, Father Maximilian returned to Poland and began his missionary activities. He published a monthly magazine called *The Knights of the Immaculata* and in 1927 founded the "City of the Immaculata," where over seven hundred friars, totally consecrated to Mary, devoted themselves to various evangelization activities, including the Apostolate of the Printed Word.

In 1930, moved by a desire to lead the whole world to Christ through Mary, Saint Maximilian traveled to Japan and established a second City of the Immaculata close to Nagasaki. During World War II, Nagasaki's City of the Immaculata was spared annihilation from the atom bomb, and was used as a hospital and center for thousands of refugees, including Jews. Saint Maximilian was arrested and imprisoned in the Pawiak

Prison, near Warsaw. On May 28, 1941, he was permanently transferred to the Auschwitz concentration camp, where inhumane conditions and hard labor awaited him. Maximilian, now prisoner number 16670, continued to be an instrument of love among his fellow prisoners, under the guidance of Blessed Mother Mary.

One day Maximilian freely offered his own life for a fellow prisoner who had been condemned to death in the starvation bunker. After nearly two weeks of intense suffering through a slow death, Maximilian was killed by an injection of carbolic acid, on the eve of the Solemnity of the Assumption of Our Lady, August 14, 1941. On October 10, 1982, Pope John Paul II canonized Maximilian, a saint and martyr of charity.

The Story of Saint Louis de Montfort
January 31, 1673 – April 28, 1716
(Compiled by Francesco)

Saint Louis de Montfort was a priest for sixteen years. He had been a pious child, especially devoted to prayer before the Blessed Sacrament. When the brilliant saint reached age nineteen, he gave away all that he owned and resolved to live on alms alone. He was ordained a priest in Paris and worked for some time as a hospital chaplain there, but eventually shifted his time and devotion to preaching, a task for which he was especially gifted. Saint Louis went on to found the "Daughters of Wisdom," an order devoted to hospital work and educating poor girls, and the "Company of Mary" (today called the Montfort Fathers), a missionary group of priests. It is Louis' devotion to Mary, though, for which he is most revered.

He wrote a famous formula for "Total Consecration to Mary." Saint Louis describes it as a short, smooth, sure, and perfect way to attain union with Jesus. Pope Saint John Paul II once recalled how as a young seminarian he "read and reread the writings of Saint Louis de Montfort." The pope singled out the saint's writings as the "decisive turning point" in his life. He had came to the conclusion that he could not exclude the Lord's Mother from his life without neglecting the will of God.

In Pope John Paul II's apostolic letter, *Rosarium Virginis Mariae*, (inspired by Saint Louis' doctrine on the excellence of Marian devotion and total consecration) the pope tells of his lifelong personal motto, "Totus Tuus," which means "All for you." He totally consecrated himself to Our Blessed Mother.

There are various approaches to consecration. First, we can plunge into it without certainty of what outcomes we may experience. Everyone who does the Saint Louis de Montfort consecration likely won't fully understand all that they're doing and opening themselves up to. That is the beauty of an "act of faith." Many who do this do it in trust. Our conviction is that, even though we're uncertain, we allow Mary to begin to use us in mysterious ways.

We trust that the Blessed Virgin's identity as God's beloved daughter, the Lord's Mother, and the chosen spouse of the Holy Spirit, neutralizes the risk of going forward. We may try a sort of "apprenticeship consecration," similar to being a nun in her novitiate. In this case we set aside a day, week, month, or year to discover whether consecration is suitable to our state in life. Since every human being is absolutely unique, there is really no way to grade or determine how well we are doing. That would be for the Blessed Mother to assess in collaboration with Jesus. My personal inclination is to *just do it*. Most assuredly it's suited to our lives! We can select from several versions of consecration to Our Blessed Mother. Many differing formulas are used to consecrate oneself to the Mother of God, but total consecration is best laid out in the writings of Saint Louis Marie de Montfort.

Saint Louis de Montfort's Way of Total Consecration

Saint Louis de Montfort's formula for total consecration to Mary should be taken quite seriously as a spiritual vocation for life. Read his book entitled *True Devotion to Mary*; then select a Marian feast day for the day of your consecration. His method has a three-week period of preparation.

Total Consecration to Jesus
(Through the Immaculate Heart of Mary)

Three-Week Preparation of Saint Louis de Montfort

"227. Those who desire to take up this special devotion should spend at least twelve days in emptying themselves of the spirit of the world, which is opposed to the spirit of Jesus. I recommended in the first part of this preparation for candidates to seek the reign of Jesus in their hearts. They should then spend three weeks imbuing themselves with the spirit of Jesus, through the most Blessed Virgin. Here is a program they might follow…"

Week One Preparations

"228. During the first week candidates should offer Jesus all their prayers and acts of devotion: seeking to acquire knowledge of themselves and sorrow for their sins. Let them perform all actions in a spirit of humility. With this end in view, they may wish to meditate on what I have said concerning our corrupted nature, and consider themselves during six days of the week as nothing but snails, slugs, toads, swine, snakes and goats. Or else they may meditate on the following three considerations of Saint Bernard: 'Remember what you were—corrupted seed; what you are—a body destined for decay; what you will be—food for worms.' They will ask Jesus and the Holy Spirit to enlighten them saying, 'Lord, that I may see,' or 'Lord, let me know myself,' or the 'Come, Holy Spirit.' Every day they should pray the 'Litany of the Holy Spirit.' Candidates should turn to Our Blessed Mother and beg her to obtain for them the great grace of self-knowledge. For this intention candidates will pray each day the 'Ave Maris Stella' and the 'Litany of the Blessed Virgin.'"

Week Two Preparations

"229. Each day of the second week candidates should endeavor, in all their prayers and works, to acquire an understanding of the Blessed Virgin; while asking the Holy Spirit for this grace. Candidates should read and meditate upon all they can discover about her. They should pray daily the 'Litany of the Holy Spirit' and the 'Ave Maris Stella' as during the first week. In addition, candidates will pray at least five decades of the rosary for greater understanding of Our Blessed Mother."

Week Three Preparations

"230. During the third and final week of preparation, candidates should seek to understand Jesus better. They may read and meditate on what Holy Scripture says about Him, and research all available resources about Him. Candidates may pray repeatedly the prayer of Saint Augustine: 'Lord, that I may know you,' or 'Lord, that I may see.' As during the previous week, they should recite the 'Litany of the Holy Spirit' and the 'Ave Maris Stella,' adding in the last week every day praying the 'Litany of the Holy Name of Jesus.'

"231. At the end of these three weeks, candidates should go to confession and Holy Communion; intent on consecrating themselves, to Jesus through Mary, as voluntary slaves of love. After receiving Holy Communion, candidates then recite an act of consecration. They should have it copied and sign it on the very day they enter into consecration."

Act of Consecration to Jesus through Mary

(The original with "Thee" and "Thine" retained in honor of Saint Louis de Montfort)

O Eternal and Incarnate Wisdom! O sweetest and most adorable Jesus! True God and true man, only Son of the Eternal Father, and of Mary, always virgin! I adore Thee profoundly in the bosom and splendors of Thy Father during eternity; and I adore Thee also in the virginal bosom of Mary, Thy most worthy Mother, in the time of Thine Incarnation.

I give Thee thanks for that Thou hast annihilated Thyself, taking the form of a slave in order to rescue me from the cruel slavery of the devil. I praise and glorify Thee for that Thou hast been pleased to submit Thyself to Mary, Thy Holy Mother, in all things, in order to make me Thy faithful slave through her. But, alas! Ungrateful and faithless as I have been, I have not kept the promises which I made so solemnly to Thee in my Baptism; I have not fulfilled my obligations; I do not deserve to be called Thy child, nor yet Thy slave; and as there is nothing in me which does not merit Thine anger and Thy repulse, I dare not come by myself before Thy most holy and august Majesty. It is on this account that I have recourse to the intercession of Thy Most Holy Mother, whom Thou hast given me for a mediatrix with Thee. It is through her that I hope to obtain of Thee contrition, the pardon of my sins, and the acquisition and preservation of wisdom.

Hail, then, O Immaculate Mary, living tabernacle of the Divinity, where the Eternal Wisdom willed to be hidden and to be adored by angels and by men! Hail, O Queen of Heaven and earth, to whose empire everything is subject which is under God. Hail, O sure refuge of sinners, whose mercy fails no one. Hear the desires which I have of the Divine Wisdom; and for that end receive the vows and offerings which in my lowliness I present to thee.

  I, _____, a faithless sinner, renew and ratify today in thy hands the vows of my Baptism; I renounce forever Satan, his pomps and works; and I give myself entirely to Jesus Christ, the Incarnate Wisdom, to carry my cross after Him all the days of my life, and to be more faithful to Him than I have ever been before. In the presence of all the heavenly court

I choose thee this day for my Mother and Mistress. I deliver and consecrate to thee, as thy slave, my body and soul, my goods, both interior and exterior, and even the value of all my good actions, past, present and future; leaving to thee the entire and full right of disposing of me, and all that belongs to me, without exception, according to thy good pleasure, for the greater glory of God in time and in eternity.

Receive, O Benignant Virgin, this little offering of my slavery, in honor of, and in union with, that subjection which the Eternal Wisdom deigned to have to thy maternity; in homage to the power which both of you have over this poor sinner, and in thanksgiving for the privileges with which the Holy Trinity has favored thee. I declare that I wish henceforth, as thy true slave, to seek thy honor and to obey thee in all things.

O admirable Mother, present me to thy dear Son as His eternal slave, so that as He has redeemed me by thee, by thee He may receive me! O Mother of mercy, grant me the grace to obtain the true Wisdom of God; and for that end receive me among those whom thou lovest and teachest, whom thou leadest, nourishest and protectest as thy children and thy slaves.

O faithful Virgin, make me in all things so perfect a disciple, imitator and slave of the Incarnate Wisdom, Jesus Christ thy Son, that I may attain, by thine intercession and by thine example, to the fullness of His age on Earth and of His glory in Heaven. Amen.

_____   _____
Sign your name here   Date

The Tradition of "Holy Voluntary Slavery"

We shouldn't be taken aback by the use of the term "slave" in Saint Louis de Montfort's consecration to Mary. He explains the concept of "holy voluntary slavery" very well. The word "slave" in today's culture has, of course, a very distasteful connotation. But in the days of Joseph, Mary, and Jesus the keeping of household and other slaves or "servants" was a common practice. The very lowest of slaves was the one assigned to wash the feet of guests. One day Jesus overheard his apostles arguing about which of them was the greatest. He quickly admonished them and said that if they aspired to be the greatest they must take on the role of the least and serve the rest. Before His passion and death, Jesus went so far as to wrap a towel around His waist and wash the feet of all His apostles.

At the time of her Annunciation, the Blessed Virgin responded to the Angel Gabriel by proclaiming, "I am the handmaid of the Lord, let it be done unto me according to your word." The most endearing title for every pope is "The Servant of the Servants of the Lord." The Holy Father's role is lowest of all: he is a servant who is pledged to serve servants.

One of the most curious books of the Bible is Saint Paul's Letter to Philomen. It's about Philomen's runaway slave, Onesimus, who has become a Christian brother under Saint Paul's tutelage.

The Letter of Saint Paul to Philomen
(Philemon 1:1–25)

"Paul, a prisoner for Christ Jesus, and Timothy our brother, to Philemon, our beloved and our co-worker…I urge you on behalf of my child Onesimus, whose father I have become in my imprisonment, who was once useless to you but is now useful to [both] you and me. I am sending him, that is, my own heart, back to you. I should have liked to retain him for myself, so that he might serve me on your behalf in my imprisonment for the gospel, but I did not want to do anything without your consent, so that the good you do might not be forced but voluntary. Perhaps this is why he was away from you for a while, that you might have him back forever, no longer as a slave but more than a slave, a brother, beloved especially to me, but even more so to you, as a man and in the Lord. So if you regard me as a partner, welcome him as you would me. And if he has done you any injustice or owes you anything, charge it to me. I, Paul, write this in my own hand: I will pay. May I not tell you that you owe me your very self. Yes, brother, may I profit from you in the Lord. Refresh my heart in Christ. With trust in your compliance I write to you, knowing that you will do even more than I say. At the same time prepare a guest room for me, for I hope to be granted to you through your prayers. Epaphras, my fellow prisoner in Christ Jesus, greets you, as well as Mark, Aristarchus, Demas, and Luke, my co-workers. The grace of the Lord Jesus Christ be with your spirit."

(Note by Me, Zacchaeus)

Francesco renews his consecration to the Blessed Mother each year. His usual tradition is to renew on the feast day of his original consecration in Mexico, in the city of Pueblo, on the Feast of the Immaculate Conception, December 8, 2007. He happened to notice in 2014 that the month of June was especially rich in significant feast days. It also marked the sixty-fifth birthday of his wife Bernadette, who was born on June 12. Francesco decided to renew his consecration to the Blessed Mother six months earlier than usual. Here follows Francesco's spiritual journal for June of 2014.

Francesco's Spiritual Journal for June 2014
(Renewing his consecration to the Blessed Mother)

Sunday, June 1 – Seventh Sunday of Easter

Along with following Saint Louis de Montfort's formula, I'm praying the "Brown Scapular Morning Offering," the Litanies of the Holy Spirit and Our Lady of Loreto, and the Ave Maris Stella. I discovered a beautiful version of the Ave Maris Stella on YouTube, sung in Latin with English subtitles. It takes approximately one hour to complete my morning prayers, including an online visit to televised daily Mass and the Creighton University Daily Reflection Calendar. If my timing is perfect, the clock will chime 6:00 a.m. just in time to listen to the "Regina Coeli" prayer. After morning prayers, I've been relaxing in silence. I sit outside in our backyard garden to pray the Glorious Mysteries of the rosary.

Monday, June 2 – Feast of Saints Marcellinus and Peter

I've been sleeping more soundly at night, going to bed at about 11:00 p.m. and awakening at around 5:00 a.m. I'm getting closer to refining my morning offering into something simple and peaceful. Various websites have helped provide all of Saint Louis de Montfort's prayer requirements.

This morning I visited Saint Basil's Parish in Toronto, Canada, online. The readings and the homily were very good.

I wrote a letter to a niece of mine who is graduating from Air Force basic training this month. I sent her a Miraculous Medal with a little pamphlet explaining its history.

Tuesday, June 3 – Feast of Saint Charles Lwanga and Companions

I decided to visit the EWTN daily Mass telecast at 5:00 a.m., which turned out to be a great idea. Father Joseph Mary gave a wonderful homily on the Ugandan Martyrs. My son Steve awoke and began moving about when I was about thirty minutes into a Lectio Divina session with Cardinal Collins of Toronto. He was covering the Gospel of Mark, chapter 6, in today's lesson. One thing already imprinted on my mind is the cardinal's comment about making an effort to see Christ in our most familiar places. I should seek to see Him more clearly in my son.

I missed my noon "Regina Coeli" prayer. My son came home early and we visited from about 11:30 a.m. to 4:00 p.m. in the afternoon. Although this diverted me from prayer and study, I know now that people must take precedence in our lives. The teaching of Cardinal Collins afforded me a real-life example today.

Wednesday, June 4 – *Shavout*

What is *Shavout*? It is the Jewish Festival of Weeks, which commemorates the day that the Jews received the Torah. I had quite a restful night's sleep. Today I tried a longer version of morning offerings, which included a renewal of baptismal vows, and a lengthy renewal of consecration to Our Blessed Mother.

My studies today were pretty much all on devotion to the Sacred Heart of Jesus, Saint Margaret Mary Alacoque, and the Nine First Fridays. I plan to begin that devotion this coming Friday, June 6, the anniversary of Saint Mary Alacoque's vision. I kept Steve, who was on the computer much of the afternoon job searching, in my prayers.

Thursday, June 5 – Feast of Saint Boniface

I'd love to wake up refreshed every morning like I did today at 4:30 a.m., a perfect time to make my morning offering and tune in to the 5:00 a.m. daily Mass on EWTN. Father Leonard Mary was on fire in his homily. The gospel reading of John, chapter 17, was absolutely wonderful.

I enjoyed praying all four rosaries today, especially the Luminous Mysteries in our backyard garden. I was very satisfied in my studies for tomorrow's First Friday Devotions. I'm looking forward to a Holy Hour tonight at 11:00 p.m. If all goes according to my wishes, I'll get an early start tomorrow and leave the house at around 6:30 a.m. First Friday Mass, at Saint Mary's in Vacaville, begins at 8:00 a.m. There will be adoration of the Blessed Sacrament well into the evening.

First Friday, June 6 – Feast of Saint Norbert

I had time to read Pope Pius XII's encyclical on devotion to the Sacred Heart of Jesus before leaving the house. I'm excited to observe First Friday Devotions at Saint Mary's this morning. I wanted to have a three-hour devotion from 7:00 a.m. to 10:00 a.m., starting from the moment I drove out of my driveway, to the moment I left the parish parking lot. It pretty much turned out that way. Saint Mary's has a full-blown observation of First Friday Devotions and Benediction.

First Saturday, June 7
(Day #9 of the Holy Spirit Novena)

I discovered a wonderful Lectio Divino website, by the Carmelites, which uses the daily Mass readings. The EWTN televised Mass, with Father Anthony Mary as homilist, provided a unique look at the gospel readings. There's a definite contrast between the followers of Christ in active and contemplative roles. Saints Peter and John were the examples from today's gospel, but others, like Martha and Mary, come to mind. My own relationship and partnership with my wife Bernadette is very similar. Father Anthony Mary emphasized that we need a balance of both features in our lives.

This morning was day #9 of my Holy Spirit Novena. I feel well disposed to celebrate Pentecost tomorrow since attending First Saturday Devotions at Saint Joseph Parish in Vacaville. Their daily Mass chapel has a distinct feature: it seats a capacity of 120, the number of people which Scripture records as being present in the "upper room" at Pentecost.

Sunday, June 8 – Feast of Pentecost

It was the first time in many months that I attended Holy Mass at my home parish, Saint Peter's. (I'm a wandering vagabond.) We have a new pastor, Father Mike. I had a nice visit with one of our Eucharistic ministers and also a choir member. After Mass I visited with a woman who lives on my street, and with our soon-to-be deacon, who will be ordained on June 28, the Memorial of the Immaculate Heart; this is also the day I intend to renew my consecration to Our Blessed Mother.

I'm hoping to learn to sing the Salve Regina by heart this month. I found a very nice version on YouTube with Latin and English subtitles. This will be a joyful song to sing in the shower.

Monday, June 9 – Feast of Saint Ephrem
(First Week of Consecration Renewal Preparations)

Saint Louis de Montfort tells me to reflect and focus on five aspects of prayer this week. 1) To offer all my devotions to acquire knowledge of myself and sorrow for my sins. 2) To contemplate my human disposability after death, in order to foster a spirit of humility. 3) To ask the Holy Spirit for enlightenment by frequently employing three short supplications throughout the day: "Lord, that I may know myself"; "Lord, that I may see"; and "Come Holy Spirit." 4) To ask Our Blessed Mother for the grace of self-knowledge. 5) To recite each day the Ave Maris Stella and the Litany of the Blessed Virgin of Loreto.

I was much absorbed in my reflections this morning, and fairly exhausted mentally and emotionally by 9:00 a.m.

Meditations one and two of Saint Francis de Sales on "Origins as Creatures" proved very enlightening. I had to make several "side trips" to research the thoughts that came to me, including the human development cycle in a mother's womb. In my little inspirations, I saw that the nine months in my mother's womb were like a novena of sorts representing total dependence. I was fascinated during my contemplation of reality before I existed. There is so much human history, including Holy Church history, to consider. One reassuring lesson I learned today is that we are privileged to be the highest in the order of creatures in God's material creation.

Tuesday, June 10
(First Week of Consecration Renewal Preparations)

Saint Louis de Montfort says to present myself to Jesus with a spirit of true sorrow for my sins, through Our Blessed Mother's Immaculate Heart. This cannot be merely an intellectual venture, but must be a true act of love. Here's where the difficulty lies. In many ways, I'm beginning to see that the gift of true devotion to the Blessed Virgin Mary and the Sacred Heart of Jesus is one that requires an authentic calling. Being now present at this juncture and still falling short of absolute confidence in faith, I hope I'm called. *Lord, help me to believe.*

The three specific prayers Saint Louis directs us to pray during week #1 of preparation are the Litany of the Holy Spirit, the Ave Maris Stella, and the Litany of Loreto. I don't think he intended for us to skip our usual morning offerings, midday, or evening prayers. I'm having fun learning to sing the Salve Regina in Latin by heart. I sense that it will be pleasing to Our Blessed Mother.

My meditations on "knowing myself" were very fruitful today. One thing I learned is that God is "stuck with me." Because He loves us so much, He will never cease loving us. One important thing to keep in mind is that, on the cross, Jesus said to just one of the thieves, "Today you will be with me in paradise."

Wednesday, June 11 – Feast of Saint Barnabas
(First Week of Consecration Renewal Preparations)

I see from my meditations on self that God truly created us in His own image. The love He now has for humanity far surpasses any love we can ever have for Him. His love is so surpassing that we will forever possess free will.

I wonder if God is sorrowful in His love for us. His sorrows must come when we separate ourselves from His divine will. Luisa Piccarreta, the "Little Daughter of the Divine Will," was very helpful to me in my evening meditations. Our earthly personas, separated from our immortal souls, Luisa says, are essentially worthless. She contends that all our experiences, encounters, thoughts, words, deeds, and choices, apart from the Divine Will, have no value whatsoever. We may live our natural purpose "with love," but still fall short of God's purpose if we fail to desire His divine will, or worse, if we do not even pay attention to His will. Fortunately, often without knowing, we've probably managed to please God from time to time.

A small stumbling block concerning Our Blessed Mother was clarified for me in prayer today. In her Magnificat she proclaimed, "My soul rejoices in God my Savior." Therefore I'm no longer confused regarding her title of Co-Redemptrix.

She is merely the sacred vessel containing the Blessed Sacrament, so to speak. She in no way is placed on equal status with her beloved Son. Regardless, many millions of souls have gone through her Immaculate Heart on a pathway to redemption. We know one thing for sure: God Himself described her as "full of grace" long before He dwelt in her womb.

Thomas Merton suggested four emotions to meditate upon throughout the day: Love, Fear, Joy, and Sorrow. I added Anger and Hate.

Thursday, June 12 – Bernadette's Sixty-Fifth Birthday

(First Week of Consecration Renewal Preparations)

I center my meditations today on the intellect and the emotional outbursts of anger and jealousy. It's advisable to complete all spiritual tasks even though we feel physically and mentally drained.

Having difficulties, for most of the day, in concentrating on my prayers for consecration renewal, I decided to partake of some fun diversions and listened for a good length of time to gospel music. My favorite selections were the Soweto Gospel Choir performing "Oh Happy Day" and a Ray Charles' rendition of the same song. I'm still enjoying trying to learn the Salve Regina by heart. I've mastered the first half so far.

Friday, June 13 – Feast of Saint Anthony of Padua

(First Week of Consecration Renewal Preparations)

This first week of consecration renewal preparations focused on "self-knowledge," and meditating on my human nature, specifically my physical, emotional, and intellectual properties. I keep recalling what Luisa Piccarreta said: "All things outside the Divine Will have no meaning." Saint Louis de Montfort said that I must imbue myself with the Spirit of Jesus, through the most Blessed Virgin. Although I didn't initially comprehend this, my week of prayer has brought me to a place of better clarity.

I was just in time to watch the EWTN televised Mass at 5:30 a.m. Father Anthony Mary was celebrant, and gave a wonderful homily on Saint Anthony of Padua, his patron saint. I especially enjoyed the story of the donkey and the Holy Eucharist. I discovered a 1931 silent movie, on the life of Saint Anthony, on YouTube.

Saturday, June 14

(First Week of Consecration Renewal Preparations)

Throughout the entire week I received heavenly help in my meditations. I contemplated my physical nature, the seven senses, my emotions, and my intellect. I thoroughly considered who and what I am. As I mentioned before, my most reassuring conclusion is that God, due to His immeasurable love for me, is pretty much "stuck with me." He loves us so much that He's made us in His own image. We are the highest order of His material creatures.

Sometime around midday, I reflected on my life roles, my various occupations, and my endeavors. I graded myself according to how well I aligned myself to the Divine Will as I went about my various activities. It was not a laudable assessment. There are only a few areas where I receive an "A" rating. Still, it was good to recall the many human endeavors I've involved myself with over time. Various homilies I've heard, and studies I engaged in this week, remind me of the simple purpose we have in life: to know, love, and serve God and one another.

Sunday, June 15 – Feast of the Most Holy Trinity

(First Week of Consecration Renewal Preparations)

Saint Louis' daily prayer requirements remain the same for week #2. All studies and prayers are to be focused on Our Blessed Mother. I'm overwhelmed as to where to begin my studies of the Blessed Virgin Mary. Encyclicals, and the Catechism for sure, can be a starting point. There's far too much written about Our Blessed Mother to cover in one short week. Her titles alone number well in the hundreds. I found a Marian calendar that relates a title or honor of Our Blessed Mother for every day of the year. I hope to begin visiting this website on a frequent basis. I've chosen two movies and six lectures on Our Blessed Mother, to help in getting to know her better throughout the week. However, I believe that silence, quiet time, and contemplation through her most holy rosary will prove most fruitful.

Monday, June 16 – Eleventh Week in Ordinary Time
(Second Week of Consecration Renewal Preparations)

The first day of study and meditation on Our Blessed Mother has been very encouraging. My morning offerings and early activities are flowing very well. I began by listening to the hymn "Holy, Holy, Holy." It was the entrance song used at yesterday's Solemnity of the Blessed Trinity Mass. Today's study "menu" covered the Blessed Mother's perfect faith and obedience. I prayed a very nice Joyful Mysteries rosary with help from Father Peter John Cameron's lecture on "The Mysteries of Mary." It was part of an EWTN program hosted by Father Mitch Pacwa. I also studied several sections of the Catechism on Our Blessed Mother.

Tuesday, June 17 – Eleventh Week in Ordinary Time
(Second Week of Consecration Renewal Preparations)

Two things stood out in the several homilies and lectures I listened to today. "God wills us to be in the likeness and image of His Son, so who better than the Blessed Mother to show us how to attain this grace." "Christ on the cross is the new Tree of Life in the new Garden of Eden, and Our Blessed Mother is the New Eve." I had a nice conversation with Our Blessed Mother in the backyard garden, praying the Sorrowful Mysteries of the rosary. Not even the chirping birds entered my ears. I realize that the Lord of our redemption lovingly dispenses His mercy to us all. He, however, was shown no mercy in His passion. I was directed somehow to read Pope Francis' apostolic exhortation *Evangelii Guadium*.

Wednesday, June 18 – Eleventh Week in Ordinary Time

(Second Week of Consecration Renewal Preparations)

Father Mark Mary (celebrating the EWTN televised daily Mass today) clarified why I was anxious to read Pope Francis' exhortation. The gospel readings for this period are on the Sermon on the Mount, and the Holy Father's *Evangelii Guadium* is much like a modern-day presentation of the Lord's Sermon on the Mount.

Thursday, June 19 – Feast of Saint Romuald

(Second Week of Consecration Renewal Preparations)

Sacred Heart Novena, Day #1
(For the Intentions of Jim and Louise)

I paid a visit to Cache Creek Indian Casino yesterday afternoon and talked with one of the employees, named Sherwin, a Guyana immigrant. Sherwin first came to Yuba City to live with an aunt before bringing his family to join him. When I saw him, he seemed to be falling asleep on his feet, so I asked him if he wanted a cup of coffee to wake up. He told me the story of his moving from Yuba City to Sacramento, and how he then came to work at the casino for his 2:30 a.m. to 10:30 a.m. shift. I asked Sherwin to thank God for his recent blessings: his citizenship and his passing the probation period at Cache Creek Casino. He has graduated with a bachelor's degree in electronics from Chico State University.

I studied chapter 2 of *Evangelii Guadium* when I came home. I completed chapter 3 this evening. The gospel in today's Mass reminded me of the silence and simplicity needed in our prayer lives. I began praying a novena to the Sacred Heart of Jesus this morning for the intentions of my friends, Jim and Louise.

Friday, June 20 – Sacred Heart Novena, Day #2

(Second Week of Consecration Renewal Preparations)

"Our heavenly Father knows what we want before we ask Him." So said Jesus just before He taught us to pray the "Lord's Prayer." I hope to be more simple and quiet in my studies and prayer. Taking this advice of the Lord to heart, I spent the first five waking hours of this day in silence and openness to God's grace. I am very much refreshed.

Saturday, June 21 – Sacred Heart Novena, Day #3
(Second Week of Consecration Renewal Preparations)

After completing my morning offering and watching the Sydney Australia daily televised Mass, I finished reading *Evangelii Guadium*. I confess that it was sometimes tedious to go through its 288 paragraphs. But I see clearly why I was directed to read Pope Francis' first exhortation on the Joy of the Gospel. I feel in my heart that Our Blessed Mother is herself the Joy of the Gospel. Like the sacraments instituted by our Lord to give grace, she is herself a living sacrament and the Dispenser of All Graces.

My sister sent me a beautiful and mysterious postcard from Taos, New Mexico, telling the story of a painting by Henri Ault, which can be found in the little chapel of Saint Francis. The painting is entitled "The Shadow of the Cross." I came to realize that Our Blessed Mother stood in the shadow of the cross when her Son took His last breath. The eight-foot-in-size painting has a very interesting history behind it.

Today is the last day of my second week of preparation for my consecration renewal. The week-long meditation on Our Blessed Mother was very rewarding. I must call on the Holy Spirit for guidance on the upcoming week of meditating on Jesus.

Sunday, June 22 – Feast of the Most Holy Body and Blood of Christ (Corpus Christi Sunday)

(Second Week of Consecration Renewal Preparations)

Sacred Heart Novena, Day #4

Today's Feast of Corpus Christi was one of those days which needed extra preparation. Bernadette and I attended eight-thirty Mass at Saint Peter's. The celebrant, Father Mike, gave his personal witness. He was a young soldier in the 1990s Gulf War. He happened to be invited by the combatant priest to celebrate Mass with a small group, on the tailgate of a jeep, amidst the ongoing surroundings of war. Mike received Holy Communion, as a true believer in the presence of our Lord in the Blessed Sacrament, and continued for several months to receive the Blessed Sacrament. Upon returning to California, after the war, Mike inquired of a priest how to officially become Catholic. He innocently confided that he'd been receiving Holy Communion for months. The priest corrected Mike's error and enrolled him in the RCIA program. In 1991, Mike received his first "licit" Holy Communion. Part two of the story: Mike was ordained a Catholic priest in 2004. In Father Mike's homily, on the Feast of Corpus Christi, he expressed perplexity at the sad fact that the world in general (even within Holy Mother Church) does not recognize the True Presence. My prayerful focus in Week #3 of my consecration renewal preparations will be on the Body and Blood of Christ in the Blessed Sacrament.

I've come close to forgetting to pray the novena to the Sacred Heart of Jesus for Jim and Louise's intentions. I must put a string around my finger or a large note on the computer screen.

Sarah visited today, and did the cooking for lunch and her laundry. We've missed the visits of our son-in-law, Anthony, who has been working Sundays as of late.

Monday, June 23 – Twelfth Week in Ordinary Time
(Final Week of Consecration Renewal Preparations)

Sacred Heart Novena, Day #5

My morning offering, watching of the televised Mass, and praying the novena to the Sacred Heart were all wrought with distraction. I partially blame my flare-up of arthritis (in my right hand) and being too hungry at 5:00 a.m. The true culprit, however, is my lack of patience. My first study source for this week's meditations on Jesus is *The Original Catholic Encyclopedia*.

Contemplative praying of the most holy rosary has been more than satisfying. In relation to Christ our Lord, Our Blessed Mother is the most perfect disciple, fully embracing the purpose of discipleship, and continuing the work of her Son for the whole of humanity.

Tuesday, June 24 – Nativity of Saint John the Baptist

(Final Week of Consecration Renewal Preparations)

Sacred Heart Novena, Day #6

The David Haas Music of Praise Medley was a very soothing end to a long day of study and prayer. I learned several things about our Lord in today's readings. My studies led me to an EWTN program from September of 2007, which included a talk by a Franciscan friar, Father Benedict Groeschel, on the Holy Eucharist. His talk, in turn, led me to two writings by Pope Benedict XVI and Saint Pope John Paul II (*Sacramentum Caritatis* and *Ecclesia Eucharistia*).

My reflections on the holy rosary, and "conversations" with Our Blessed Mother, continue to bring me very uplifting inspirations. This final week of preparations focuses on the person of Jesus, both on His human and divine nature. My anticipation is mounting as I come closer to June 28, the day I plan to renew my consecration to Our Blessed Mother.

Wednesday, June 25 – Twelfth Week in Ordinary Time

(Final Week of Consecration Renewal Preparations)

Sacred Heart Novena, Day #7

    I prayed the morning offering according to Saint Louis' directions and visited an EWTN taped program interview with two priests advocating perpetual adoration. The interview revealed some striking facts about adoration of the Blessed Sacrament. I believe that the main stumbling block in desiring closeness to the Eucharist is our lack of faith. I think that the disciples could not stay awake with Jesus for one hour because they weren't absolutely certain He was the Christ. I believe we have the same dilemma today: we are not fully convinced of the True Presence, so it becomes much more difficult to attend a Holy Hour. The priest being interviewed reminded me of one of the most beautiful prayers from Holy Mass: "By this mingling of water and wine may we come to share in the Divinity of Christ, who humbled Himself to share in our humanity." As always, faith remains a gift from God.

    My hopes to finish reading the "Fourth Gospel," that is, the letters to the Romans, Galatians, and Corinthians, is stalled. I only managed to get through four chapters of the Book of Romans. I'm becoming more and more excited as my consecration renewal to Our Blessed Mother on June 28 approaches.

Thursday, June 26 – Twelfth Week in Ordinary Time

(Final Week of Consecration Renewal Preparations)

Sacred Heart Novena, Day #8

Tomorrow will be the Feast of the Sacred Heart of Jesus, and this Saturday is the Feast of the Immaculate Heart of Mary. There is no more time to frantically search for answers and knowledge. It is time to reflect on what I have discerned over the past three weeks.

Once I renew my consecration on Saturday, I hope to simplify much of my prayer day. I hope to enjoy study by bouncing back and forth between lectures and homilies, but I hope to limit myself there as well. I hope to read and study only the best.

Friday, June 27 – Feast of the Sacred Heart

(Final Day of Consecration Renewal Preparations)

Sacred Heart Novena, Final Day

I completed my Sacred Heart novena, for the intentions of my friend Jim, who's undergoing prostate cancer treatment. He will also celebrate his seventieth birthday on July 1.

Father Collin celebrated a very wonderful solemn Mass for the Sacred Heart of Jesus at 8:00 a.m. Many of my old Saint Peter's friends were present.

Saturday, June 28 – Memorial of the Virgin Mary's Immaculate Heart

(Consecration Renewal to Our Blessed Mother)

I am renewed in consecration to the Sacred Heart of Jesus, through the Immaculate Heart of the Blessed Virgin Mary! "Oh Blessed Mother of God, make my heart like yours."

The Venerable Pope Pius XII said, "The devotion to the Sacred Heart of Jesus is the foundation on which to build the kingdom of God in the hearts of individuals, families and nations."

Father Ignatius Manfredonia, of Our Lady of Guadalupe Friary, spoke of the union of the Two Hearts of Jesus and Mary:

> On the day after we celebrated the solemnity of the Sacred Heart of Jesus, it's fitting that we observe the Feast of the Immaculate Heart of Mary; to show the union of these two hearts…as Saint Pope John Paul II used to say, the "Alliance of the Hearts of Jesus and Mary."…The Hearts of Jesus and Mary were united from the beginning until the end. At the Annunciation, at the moment of conception, and at the foot of the cross, when Jesus' Sacred Heart was pierced by a lance, and Mary's Immaculate Heart was "pierced by a sword." The whole purpose of our devotion to the Immaculate Heart of Mary is to enable us to love the Sacred Heart of Jesus with the same intensity by which the Blessed Mother herself loves Him in her Immaculate Heart.

Sunday, June 29 – Solemnity of Saints Peter and Paul

(Day After Renewed Consecration)

Yesterday concluded for me a very exhausting but exciting seven-week formation to renew my consecration to Our Blessed Mother.

My older brother Mike and I had our usual Sunday morning visit by phone. Both of us have been corresponding with a great niece who's just now graduated from Air Force basic training. Mike sent an airline ticket and hotel reservations to Lauren's mother Elizabeth (our brother Joe's daughter) so she could attend the graduation. (Very generous of Mike.) We both received nice letters from these nieces.

It has been a good time for restoring my energy and tranquility of mind. I'm looking forward to a new year under the Blessed Mother's protection and guidance.

Monday, June 30

The First Martyrs of the Holy Roman Church

I hope to restore some order into my spiritual day this July of 2014. Silence and simplicity is my goal for all my prayer sessions. I've decided to ignore the earthly clock and begin my spiritual day whenever I wake, no matter what the time. I hope to embrace three priorities for the day: to enter into God's presence, especially in my first waking hour, and renew my desire to be in union with His divine will; to attend Holy Mass and receive the Holy Eucharist; and to pray a contemplative rosary.

After Consecration
(According to Saint Louis de Montfort)

Once you have consecrated yourself to Jesus through Mary, live that consecration. Saint Louis Marie de Montfort recommended the following:

Keep praying to develop a "great contempt" for the spirit of this world.

- Maintain a special devotion to the Mystery of the Incarnation (for example, through meditation, spiritual reading, and focusing on feasts celebrating the Incarnation, such as the Annunciation and the Nativity).
- Frequently recite the Ave Maris Stella, the rosary, and the Magnificat.
- Recite, every day if it is not inconvenient, the "Little Crown of the Blessed Virgin" which is a series of Pater Nosters, Ave Marias, and Glorias; there is one Ave Maria for each star in the Virgin's crown. (Saint Louis has a special way of praying the Little Crown, which is recommended.)
- Do everything through, with, in, and for Mary, for the sake of Jesus, with the prayer, "I am all yours Immaculate One, with all that I have: in time and in eternity," in your heart and on your lips.
- Associate yourself with Mary in a special way before, during, and after Holy Communion.
- Wear a little iron chain (around the neck, wrist, waist, or ankle) as an outward sign and reminder of holy slavery. (This practice is optional, but strongly recommended by Saint Louis.) The description of this chain is not further specified.

- Renew the consecration once a year on the same date chosen above, by following the same three-week period of exercises. If desired, also renew the consecration monthly with the prayer, "I am all yours and all I have is yours, O dear Jesus, through Mary, Your Holy Mother."

Francesco's Summarization

Consecration to the Blessed Virgin Mary is not a radical departure from the ordinary affairs of our daily lives. We remain grounded in our simple definition of sainthood: "To be who we are and to be that well." It needn't interfere with our human responsibilities in life. Begin with the Mother of God's instructions at the wedding of Cana, "Do whatever He tells you to do." We find "what Jesus tells us to do" in Holy Scripture, in the spiritual writings of the saints, in homilies of holy bishops, priests, and deacons, and in our own prayerful inspirations, just to name a few. The Blessed Virgin Mary has regularly made personal appearances throughout the life of the Church. In these apparitions, she's asked us to pray, sometimes to fast, and also to do other acts of atonement. Consecrated to her, it becomes our obligation to study and discover exactly what her various requests have been throughout time.

The Many Titles and Devotions of the Blessed Virgin Mary

(Thoughts by Me, Zacchaeus)

Francesco recently discovered the "Marian Calendar," which provides details of apparitions and other celebrated honors of the Mother of God for every day of the year. If Francisco had his way, this next section on the many titles of Mary would be over a thousand pages long. It seems that every month Francesco acquires a new favorite title of Our Lady. His current favorite is Our Lady of Pompeii. This you will have to look up yourself, otherwise we'd be on the road to a thousand pages.

The Virgin Mary has appeared under, and been honored with, hundreds of titles. Here are just fifteen of them:

Mary the Mother of God

The Blessed Virgin Mary

The Immaculate Conception

Our Lady of the Assumption

Mary Queen of Peace

Mary Queen of All Saints

Our Lady of the Miraculous Medal

Our Lady of Perpetual Help

Our Lady of Mount Carmel

Our Lady of the Snows
Our Lady of Sorrows
Our Lady of Knock
Our Lady of Guadalupe
Our Lady of Lourdes
Our Lady of Fatima

Mary the Mother of God

Mary's title as "Mother of God" is the oldest and highest of all. God Himself explicitly states this when His messenger, the Archangel Gabriel, explains to the perplexed Virgin of Nazareth that her Child will be conceived by the Holy Spirit and be called the Son of the Most High. Also, the mother of John the Baptist greets her by proclaiming, "Who am I that the Mother of my Lord should come to me?" Mary is undoubtedly what the earliest disciples of Jesus and the Church to this day have called her: *Theotokos*, which is Greek for "The Mother of God."

Apostolic succession has indeed left an unbroken trail of honor and veneration toward the Mother of God, not for any need of proof or verification for her identity, but a natural loving happenstance, beginning, perhaps, at the foot of the cross. The early evangelists and writers of Sacred Scripture mention quite often that "the Mother of the Lord was there."

I, Francesco, have known the Blessed Mother as my Holy Mother since I was a child. My grandfather, Louis, and my mother, Jean, told me of her. One of the earliest prayers I learned was, of course, the Hail Mary.

To settle all challenges on the matter, Mary was dogmatically declared the mother of Jesus, who is God, in the very city where Mary had lived for several years, at the Council of Ephesus in 431 A.D.

The Blessed Virgin Mary

The perpetual virginity of Mary is expressed in a threefold manner: in her virginal conception of Christ, in giving birth to Christ, and her continued virginity after His birth.

The Catechism of the Catholic Church, carrying the seal of Pope Benedict XVI, expounds on this in paragraphs 396 and 510. This triple statement expressing the fullness of this mystery of faith was beautifully taught by Saint Augustine (354–430 A.D.), Saint Peter Chrysologus (circa 400–450 A.D.), and Pope Saint Leo the Great (440–461 A.D.).

The deepening of faith in Mary's virginal motherhood led the Church to confess Mary's real and perpetual virginity even in the act of giving birth to Jesus. In fact, His birth "didn't diminish the Blessed Mother's virginal integrity but sanctified it." And so the liturgy of the Church celebrates Mary as *Aeiparthenos*, the "Ever-Virgin." (Note: The "brothers" of Jesus mentioned in Scripture are His kinsmen. In the Hebrew language there was no word for cousin, or half-brother, or step-brother; all were referred to under the Hebrew word for brother. The Greek word used to designate Jesus' brothers (*adelphos*) is the same word used for His kinsmen, such as Saints James and John of Zebedee, all "brothers" in the faith. This is important to know.)

The Immaculate Conception

When Saint Bernadette asked the beautiful lady at Lourdes who she was, the Blessed Mother said, "I am the Immaculate Conception." Pope Pius IX, in 1854, proclaimed it to be a dogma of the Catholic Faith. This is to me, Francesco, a no-brainer. How could the Blessed Mother be "full of grace" and have the "Lord with her," as the Archangel said, unless she was the one human being singularly gifted as being free of Original Sin?

Our Lady of the Assumption

That Mary's body did not experience corruption but was assumed into heaven was defined as a dogma by Pope Pius XII in 1950. According to the Catechism of the Catholic Church, paragraph 974: "The Most Blessed Virgin Mary, when the course of her earthly life was completed, was taken up body and soul into the glory of heaven, where she already shares in the glory of her Son's Resurrection, anticipating the resurrection of all members of his Body."

Mary Queen of Peace

Devotion to Our Blessed Mother, Queen of Peace is on the rise. A magnificent thirty-three-foot stainless steel statue by world-renowned sculptor Charles C. Parks was dedicated by Bishop Michael Saltarelli, on Saturday, May 26, 2007. It stands alongside Holy Spirit Church in New Castle, Delaware, and is visible to all who travel over the Delaware Memorial Bridge and Interstate 295. Search Google for the history of the statue of Our Lady Queen of Peace for the rest of the story.

Our Lady of Peace is the patroness of the Congregation of the Sacred Hearts of Jesus and Mary, a religious order founded by Peter Coudrin in Paris during the French Revolution. When the Congregation of the Sacred Hearts of Jesus and Mary brought the Catholic Faith to Hawaii, they consecrated the Hawaiian Islands under the protection of Our Lady of Peace. They erected the first Roman Catholic church in Hawaii to her. Today, the Cathedral of Our Lady of Peace in Honolulu is the oldest Roman Catholic cathedral in continuous use in the United States.

MARY QUEEN OF ALL SAINTS

The Blessed Virgin Mary, who always enjoyed the fullness of God's presence in her soul, was created sinless and is venerated in heaven as the Mother of God and Queen of All Saints. After a most holy life and death, the Blessed Virgin Mary was gloriously assumed into heaven, soul and body, and was crowned Queen of Heaven by her Son. Mary is Queen because her Son is Jesus, Our Lord. Jesus is our King because He redeemed us by dying for us on the cross. The Blessed Virgin is our Queen because she has a very special part in our redemption. She now helps in giving to people the graces merited by her Son.

Saint Bernard says, "It is the will of God that we should have all things through Mary." The saints also have received the graces they needed to become saints through her prayers. She is truly the Queen of All Saints. Pope Pius XII instituted the Feast of the Queenship of Mary, which is celebrated on August 22.

OUR LADY OF THE MIRACULOUS MEDAL

Saint Bernardine wrote: "All graces are dispensed by Mary's hands to whomever she wishes, whenever she wishes, and in whatever way she wishes." That assertion was beautifully demonstrated by the Blessed Virgin nearly four centuries later, when she appeared in Paris to a humble Sister of Charity, Catherine Labouré. It was November of 1830. It was a period when God and His Church were being attacked by His enemies, and ignored by the faithful.

Our Lady told Sister Catherine about the evils of the world, which were to become more intense in the years that lay ahead. She then portrayed an image signifying her Immaculate Conception. She instructed Sister Catherine to have a medal made to that likeness, which should be worn by all as a safeguard against the snares of the devil. As Sister Catherine tells it:

The Blessed Virgin was standing on a globe, and her face was beautiful beyond words. Her fingers were covered with precious jewels whose light dazzled me. And I heard: "Behold the symbol of the graces I shed upon those who ask for them!" Then an oval frame formed around the Blessed Virgin and I read in letters of gold: "O Mary, conceived without sin, pray for us who have recourse to thee." The vision reversed and I beheld the letter "M" surmounted by a cross, at the foot of the cross, a bar, and below all, the Heart of Jesus crowned with thorns, and the Heart of Mary pierced with a sword. A voice said to me, "Have a medal struck after this model. Persons who wear it will receive great graces, especially if they wear it around the neck."

With approval of the Church, the first of these medals were made in 1832 and were distributed in Paris. Almost immediately the blessings that Mary had promised began to shower down on those who wore her medal. The devotion spread like wildfire. Marvels of grace and health, peace and prosperity, followed in its wake. Before long people were calling it the "Miraculous" Medal. In 1836, a canonical inquiry undertaken at Paris declared the apparitions to be genuine.

Our Lady of Perpetual Help

The icon of Our Lady of Perpetual Help is perhaps the oldest icon of the Blessed Virgin. According to tradition, Saint Luke created an icon of Our Lady while she was still living in Jerusalem.

When Mary saw the beautiful icon of herself holding the Child Jesus in her arms, she blessed both the artist and his work proclaiming, "My grace will accompany this icon." The passage of centuries has proven that Mary did not forget this promise. So numerous were the miracles and favors granted by means of this holy icon that Pope Innocent III, in the year 1207, stated that Mary's soul seemed to have entered into this icon since it was so beautiful and so miraculous.

When Saint Luke completed the icon, tradition tells us he gave it to his personal friend and patron, Theophilus. In the middle of the fifth century, Saint Pulcheria erected a shrine in its honor in Constantinople. The icon remained there for a thousand years, where it was venerated by kings and emperors, saints and sinners, rich and poor, as the source of many graces.

Our Lady of Perpetual Help is widely venerated by Filipino Catholics and is informally known in their country as the *Holy Virgin of Baclaran*. A German copy of the icon is venerated in the National Shrine of Our Mother of Perpetual Help in Baclaran, Parañaque, Metro Manila. Pope John Paul II once said Mass at the shrine when he was a cardinal, and later prayed before the icon during his first pastoral visit to the country in February of 1981.

All Catholic churches and chapels in the Philippines enshrine a replica of the icon, often on a side altar, with many congregations holding recitations of the rosary and the icon's associated novena, as well as Benediction and Holy Mass, every Wednesday in its honor. Devotees today still use the same novena booklet first published by the priests who introduced the icon and its devotion to the Philippines in the 1900s.

OUR LADY OF MOUNT CARMEL

On July 16, 1261, Our Lady appeared to Saint Simon Stock, a father of the Carmelite order, and presented him with the scapular. Saint Simon's story begins when he was an English Hermit that lived in the hollow of a tree. He received the name "Stock" because he lived in the hollowed trunk or stock of a tree. In time he became a Carmelite and later the father general of the order. He led the order during a time of great struggles.

The Carmelites were originally hermits on Mount Carmel, near Nazareth, in the Holy Land. When they migrated to Europe, some decided to no longer be hermits and instead became friars who worked among the people. Saint Simon guided them through this transition. In the year 1251 a miraculous vision took place. Saint Simon, newly transplanted to England, prayed fervently to Our Lady.

Mary's Promise to Those Who Wear the Scapular

Our Lady's gift of the scapular came with this promise from her: "Receive, my son, this habit of your order. It shall be to you and to all Carmelites a privilege: that whosoever dies clothed in this will never suffer Eternal Fire. It will be a sign of salvation, a protection in danger, and a pledge of peace."

The "Sabbatine Privilege" is an important aspect of wearing the scapular. This concerns a promise made to Pope Saint John XXIII by the Blessed Mother. The pope recounted by papal letter that Our Lady of Mount Carmel appeared to him in a vision and stated regarding those who wear the scapular: "I, the Mother of Grace, will descend on the Saturday after their death and whomsoever I find in Purgatory I will free so that I may lead them to the Holy Mountain of life everlasting."

OUR LADY OF THE SNOWS

When we talk about a title of the Blessed Mother, there's usually a link to one of her many wonderful qualities or to one of her appearances.

Our Lady of the Snows has its ties to a legend of a marvelous snowfall in Rome in the year 352. Mary indicated to a wealthy but childless married couple in a dream that she wanted a church built in her honor and that the site of her church would be marked by a snowfall during the heat of summer. On the morning of August 5, a hill in Rome called the Esquiline Hill was covered with snow. All Rome recognized the summer snow as a miracle, and in the year 358, a church was built on the site. Restored and refurbished many times, it is the world-famous Basilica of Saint Mary Major.

Our Lady of Sorrows

Saint Bridget of Sweden gave us the Seven Sorrows Devotion. The Feast of Our Lady of Sorrows falls on September 15. The prayers honoring the Seven Sorrows, however, are prayed by devotees throughout the year. The devotion is similar to the holy rosary in that it consists of seven "Mysteries" to be meditated upon. These are the Seven Sorrows of Mary, the "great piercings" that she received throughout her life in following her Son Jesus perfectly. In our meditations on the Seven Sorrows, we pray to imitate the disposition and virtues of Our Blessed Mother, particularly in the moments of her greatest occasions of suffering.

The Seven Sorrows in Scripture

In practice: each sorrow is meditated upon while reciting one Our Father and seven Hail Marys.

The First Sorrow: The Prophecy of Simeon
  Luke 2:22–35

The Second Sorrow: The Flight into Egypt
  Matthew 2:13–21

The Third Sorrow: Jesus Lost in the Temple
  Luke 2:41–50

The Fourth Sorrow: Encounter on the Way of the Cross
  Luke 23:26–31

The Fifth Sorrow: Jesus Dies on the Cross
Mark 15:22; John 19:18, 25–27; Mark 15:34; Luke 23:46

The Sixth Sorrow: Jesus Taken Down from the Cross
John 19:31–34 and Lamentations 1:12

The Seventh Sorrow: Jesus Placed in the Tomb
Matthew 27:59; John 19:38–42; Mark 15:46; Luke 23:55–56

Our Lady of Knock

One of my neighbors, Kathy, was the first to tell me about Our Lady of Knock. She was about to leave California for Ireland after marrying an Irish dairy farmer. As a parting gift, she gave me a decorative miniature shrine with a holy water container from the shrine of Our Lady of Knock. I hurriedly looked up the story.

On a rainy night on August 21, 1879, Father Cavanaugh's housekeeper, Mary McLoughlin, went to visit a friend, Mary Beirne. On the way back to the rectory, as she approached the south gable of the church, she saw what looked like statues standing outside the buildings. When she drew closer, she recognized the Blessed Virgin Mary, Saint Joseph, and Saint John the Evangelist. Beside them and a little to the right was an altar bedecked with a cross and the figure of a lamb. She eventually realized that these were not statues, but an apparition. This event was witnessed by fifteen people ages six to sixty-five, who watched for two hours in the pouring rain while reciting the rosary. They described Our Lady as having her hands and eyes raised towards heaven as if in prayer. She was wearing, they explained, a large white cloak fastened at the neck and on her head was a brilliant crown. To her right side was Saint Joseph, head bowed and turned slightly toward her, as if offering his respects. On her left was Saint John the Evangelist, dressed as a bishop, a book in his left hand, with his right hand raised as if preaching.

Our Lady of Guadalupe

It's sometimes easy to overlook the greatness of the visionaries involved in the wonderful appearances of the Blessed Mother. Such is the case with Saint Juan Diego, most humble and worthy to be chosen by the Blessed Virgin as her personal messenger. It wasn't until April of 1990 that Juan Diego was declared blessed by Pope John Paul II and in July of 2002 he was canonized by the Church, during a ceremony celebrated by John Paul II at the Basilica of Our Lady of Guadalupe.

Saint Juan Diego was born in Mexico in 1474 and died in 1548 at age seventy-four. He lived a simple life as a weaver, farmer, and laborer. Juan was a member of the Chichimeca people (an Indian tribe). His birth name was *Cuauhtlatoatzin*, which means "the talking eagle." Between 1524 and 1525 Juan and his wife, Maria Lucia, were converted and baptized by a Franciscan priest, Father Peter da Gand, one of the first missionaries who accompanied the conquistadors.

Missionaries who first came to Mexico had little success in the beginning. After nearly a generation, only a few hundred native Mexicans had converted to the Christian faith. Christianity was not popular among the native people. Then in 1531 miracles began to happen. Jesus' own mother appeared to humble Juan Diego. On December 9, 1531, Juan rose before dawn to walk fifteen miles to Mexico City to attend daily Mass. As he passed Tepeyac Hill, he heard music and saw a glowing cloud encircled by a rainbow. A woman's voice called him to the top of the hill. There he saw a beautiful young woman dressed like an Aztec princess. She said she was the Virgin Mary and Mother of the True God. She asked Juan to tell the bishop to build a church on that site, so she could be present to help and defend those who were suffering and in pain.

When I consecrated myself to the Blessed Mother in 2007, in Mexico City, I witnessed how Our Lady of Guadalupe has gathered millions under her mantle by just arranging a few roses in a humble, devout man's *tilma*. Amazingly, she has chosen me, in an infinitely less dramatic way, to be one of her countless servants.

Our Lady of Lourdes

It's a short bus ride from Zaragoza, Spain, to Lourdes, France. I was stationed at Zaragoza with the U.S. Air Force in 1976. My wife Bernadette and I lived on the opposite side of the city's Basilica of Our Lady of the Pillar at a little neighborhood called "Nuestra Senora de Las Nieves," which means "Our Lady of the Snows." A wonderful Passionist priest, Father Pablo, lived in a monastery located directly behind our apartment building.

One morning Bernadette awakened stricken with Macular Degeneration, a form of near-complete blindness. No doctor from Spain, Germany, or the U.S. Air Force Hospital System was able to be of any help. Only the Blessed Mother could restore Bernadette's eyesight, which she did, during a pilgrimage to Lourdes with Father Pablo that year.

I watch the movie *Song of Bernadette* every year now, and never tire of the story and the reminders of the wonderful favors Our Lady bestowed on Bernadette and me.

Another miracle took place within our small busload of pilgrims from the U.S. Air Force Base at Zaragoza. A woman named Mary had been diagnosed with terminal cancer. She and her husband were making the pilgrimage to Lourdes as a last effort to seek healing. During our stay at Lourdes, Mary had an appendicitis attack and was forced to remain behind in a hospital while the rest of us, including her husband, returned to Spain. When Mary's husband was reunited with her, she had been totally cured of the cancer.

Our Lady of Fatima

The Mother of God appeared six times to three shepherd children near the town of Fatima, Portugal, between May 13 and October 13, in 1917. She told them that she had been sent by God with a message for every man, woman, and child living in our century. She promised that heaven would grant peace to all the world if her requests for prayer, reparation, and consecration were heard and obeyed.

When I retired from the U.S. Air Force in 1989, my wife Bernadette and I moved to a small town in northern California called Dixon. Next-door to the house we rented lived a lady named Gloria, a Portuguese immigrant, who cared for an elderly invalid named Gabe. Gloria was a member of the Portuguese Community of Saint Peter's Catholic Parish. A holy wedded couple named Maria and Aries attend daily Mass and sing in Portuguese the Ave Maria de Fatima song at the conclusion of the celebration.

On August 13, the anniversary of the Miracle of the Sun, they have a grand procession through the streets of town and host a great feast in honor of Our Lady. I know of no other community of men and women who so joyfully obey the entreaties of Our Lady of Fatima.

One special gift resulting from Our Blessed Mother's Fatima visit is the First Saturday Devotion. She revealed it to Sister Lucy on the evening of Thursday, December 10, 1925. It was then that the Child Jesus and the Virgin Mary visited her convent cell. Showing the young nun a heart surrounded by thorns, Our Lady said to her:

> See, My daughter, my heart surrounded by thorns which ungrateful men pierce at every moment by their blasphemies and ingratitude... Say to all those who, for five months, on the first Saturday, confess, receive Holy

Communion, recite the rosary and keep me company for fifteen minutes while meditating on the mysteries of the rosary, in a spirit of reparation, I promise to assist them at the hour of death with all the graces necessary for the salvation of their souls.

Intercession

(By Me, Zacchaeus)

Francesco prays a very nice rosary. He has the gift to imagine and visualize the twenty mysteries with ever-new "story lines." He is happy that they are "mysteries" and that he can go in so many directions. Francesco enjoys most of all praying the rosary out loud when he's driving alone in his car. He came up with a method of using his head, hands, and feet to substitute for the rosary beads and keep track of the five mysteries as he prays them.

Francesco loves to be part of the recitation of the rosary before and after Holy Mass. His most favorite public recitation is the rosary in Spanish. The prayers are more joyful to him when they are in Spanish. One of his very favorite Marian songs is "Adios Reina del Cielo," which is sung by the Spanish-speaking ladies at the conclusion of their rosary.

Through the years, Francesco has been devoted to the First Five Saturdays, and has enjoyed leading prayers of the rosary with various youth groups and single adult groups which he has sponsored. Francesco especially loves hosting a monthly "Potluck Rosary" at his house. This wonderful rosary event was rotated from house to house for many years among family and friends.

Francesco has a very fond memory of a dream he once had while stationed at an Air Force base in the early 1970s. He was napping after a particularly tiring day, and prayed himself to sleep with the Joyful Mysteries of the rosary. He heard a delightful voice in his dreams say to him, "Congratulations, Francesco, you've just prayed your one-thousandth rosary."

History and Origin of the Holy Rosary

(Compiled by Francesco)

The rosary is a form of prayer and meditation that has been around for over 1,200 years. The origin of the rosary dates back to the ninth century, when Irish monks would recite and chant the 150 psalms of the Bible as an important part of their worship. People living near the monasteries were drawn to this beautiful, harmonious devotion, and they became eager to join the monks in prayer.

Unfortunately, the people were not able to adapt to that form of prayer because psalms were very hard to memorize and printed copies of the psalms were not readily available. As a result, it was suggested to the people outside the monastery that they recite a series of 150 Our Fathers in honor of the psalms.

As this form of devotion became increasingly popular, people started to devise methods to keep track of their prayers. At first, 150 little pebbles were placed inside small leather pouches to keep count. Since this method was rather cumbersome, a thin rope having fifty knots on it was used instead, and prayed three times for a total of 150 prayers. Eventually, the method and instrument of choice became the use of string with small pieces of wood.

In later years, the Irish monks traveled throughout Europe and brought this form of devotion with them. In some areas, both clergy and lay people began to recite the "Angelic Salutation" (the first part of what we now know as the "Hail Mary") as part of the devotion. The popularity of this prayer led to the adoption of fifty Angelic Salutations being said for each piece of wood or knot on the prayer string.

During the thirteenth century, medieval theologians began to interpret the psalms as veiled mysteries about the life, death, and resurrection of Jesus. They began to write a series of psalters, or praises, in honor of Jesus for each interpretation of the psalms. In addition, 150 psalters honoring Mary were also composed.

In order to fit the existing prayer string, these psalters were divided into groups of fifty and were referred to as "rosariums." Although "rosarium" refers to roses and rose gardens, it was used to signify a collection of prayers that could be compared to a bouquet of roses.

As we see today, the rose is a very popular symbol associated with Our Blessed Mother Mary, and it is a sign that she often uses as she did in the story of Our Lady of Guadalupe.

Interpreting the psalms into written psalters lead to the implementation of special thoughts and meditations being attached to each bead. This innovated version of the rosary was widely spread by Blessed Alan de la Roche of the Dominican Order, as he revived the divinely inspired works that Saint Dominic and his rosary confraternity had initiated some hundred years earlier. The prayers of the "rosarium" were later broken down into sets of ten and these groupings became known as decades. Each decade of ten Hail Mary prayers would be preceded by one Our Father.

Around the year 1700, the meditations used in the rosary started to become narratives. Saint Louis de Montfort composed the most common set of narratives that eventually became used as meditations for each decade of the rosary. These narratives were divided into five Joyful, five Sorrowful, and five Glorious meditations that are referred to as "mysteries." In 2002, Pope

John Paul II introduced another set of five meditations referred to as the "Luminous Mysteries."

As can be seen, the rosary as we know it today is a result of many evolutions dating back several hundred years. Although the manner in which the rosary is recited or prayed has changed, the results of praying the rosary remain constant. Countless interventions still occur today, and the power and divine graces the rosary offers are available to everyone who is willing to give it a try.

Where to Find the Holy Rosary Today

The most holy rosary of the Blessed Virgin Mary can be listened to, recited, meditated upon, or contemplated. There is a wide array of "recipes" for this ancient prayer throughout the modern world, including Rosaries for Life, Scriptural Rosaries, and Special Event Rosaries. There's even a Facebook rosary (which can be found on YouTube) produced by a devotee named Roger Lacey. Roger's pleasing Irish accent, and the beautiful artwork and meditations he's put together, are truly Spirit-filled. The Eternal Word Television Network (EWTN) produced a series of all four mystery sets of the rosary, prayed by a group of young people while they tour the Holy Land. There are so many resources available to help us pray the rosary.

At virtually every Catholic parish, worldwide, (usually about half an hour before daily Mass begins) a group of women and men will recite the rosary. These devotees are soldiers for the Blessed Virgin who've helped keep the tradition on-going for generations. In many places, a "Scriptural Rosary" is prayed. Little booklets are passed out and participants take turns leading the decade prayers while reading scriptural passages. Find the

Catholic radio station for your area and you'll discover that the rosary is a regular part of their programming. Many books have been written about the holy rosary. One of many helpful websites is howtopraytherosary.com.

Keeping a Spiritual Journal

(According to Francesco)

Spiritual journals are kept, not to "blow our own horns," but to aid in remembering when we were on the right path toward God and where we may have gone wrong.

Staying the course is of most importance. The choice of formats and recording devices for our journals really shouldn't matter.

It is very important, in regard to keeping a spiritual journal, to avoid making them "activity diaries." Instead, we should share our spiritual stories in a way similar to Sacred Scripture. Our journals must become apostolic records of spiritual encounters.

Another pitfall to avoid is to beware of taking on the role of a news reporter seeking interesting stories. On any given day our journals may be as dry as can be. We simply record what the Lord brings our way. We should feel free, however, to candidly describe our emotions and all that we are. It's not of necessity to be overly specific about matters. We needn't give "spicy details" of our personal confessions.

Journals are kept as tools for improving spirituality. Once we've kept a journal for several months or more, we can reference them for insights into our journey toward holiness. As a general rule, limit daily entries to about one typed page. It's a good practice to review your journal once a week or at the end of each month.

One choice for structuring our spiritual journals is to consider three aspects of our relationship with Christ: prayer, study, and action. We can jot down a few words about our daily prayer experience, whether or not we studied anything noteworthy, and what apostolic actions we may have engaged in or encountered. Written at day's end, a concise but comprehensive spiritual journal can be employed quite effectively as our nightly examination of conscience.

Flashback to the Year 2013

(By Me, Zacchaeus)

These next several pages from Francesco's spiritual journals represent an especially exciting time for him. The year of 2013 was declared a "Year of Faith" by Pope Benedict XVI, and shortly thereafter, Pope Francis was elected to the papacy on March 13, 2013. These portions of Francesco's journal include the election of Pope Francis and Francesco's Lenten and Easter celebrations for the year.

Francesco's Spiritual Journal

January to March 2013

(Getting Ready to Celebrate the Year of Faith)

The first three days of January, 2013, were occupied by preparations for the Year of Faith, as proclaimed by his Holiness, Pope Benedict XVI. I took care of as much worldly concerns as needed attention, such as renewing my driver's license, getting my medical records in order, and refinancing my home. All these things were accomplished.

I searched my mind for a new way to organize my daily spiritual activities, and came up with an idea to simply divide the day into three eight-hour parts in honor of the Blessed Trinity. My hope is to dedicate the first and last hour of each day to prayer. These first and last hours would not necessarily be the literal first and last, but rather the hour in which I am able to give my full attention to God, both when rising and the last hour before retiring.

I will attempt to avoid my habitual sin of gluttony, by once more paying attention to correct portions and the right variety of foods. I hope to follow the advice of my doctor and moderately lose approximately five pounds per month, while eating for nutrition and health, rather than for pure pleasure and self-gratification.

Friday, January 4, 2013 – First Friday Devotions

This is the First Friday of the month for the year of 2013. I'm hoping to make the entire twenty-four hours a complete day of prayer and fasting, and to follow up with this tradition for all nine First Fridays of the year. For my meals, I propose to have only liquids, including juices, broths, and cocoa. Oh no…I already failed and binged at 10:00 p.m.

I phoned my fellow disciple John early this morning, to wish him a happy New Year in God's grace. He was on his way to a relative's funeral. Her name is Rosemary. John said that Rosemary was a very "bitter" and "unloving person" for as long as he knew her. In later life she was challenged with the death of one of her children and her husband, then ultimately her own sickness and death. I decided to dedicate my entire First Friday Devotions to Rosemary. May God bless her and fill her with grace to enter into His kingdom.

At the hospital today I had a nice talk with a sergeant who is deploying to Spain in June. I learned a great deal about him and his family. As it turned out, there is no Friday Mass at the base hospital, so I went to Saint Rose in Sacramento instead. I was able to go to confession and enjoy Mass celebrated by the Monsignor. This will be my first time attempting the nine First Friday Devotions. I've always preferred First Saturday Devotions. I brought a dozen roses and gave them to Our Blessed Mother at her little shrine of Our Lady of Guadalupe, next to the Blessed Sacrament Chapel at Saint Rose's.

January 5, 2013 – First Saturday Devotion

Today's Mass, at Saint Joseph's Parish in Vacaville, was one of those special moments given as a gift from God.

Three priests concelebrated, and a teenage altar server assisted. A very gifted organist played the "Hail Holy Queen." I arrived early for Mass and a small group was praying a scriptural Joyful Rosary. They invited me to lead the third decade. Over eighty people were at Mass, with three times more women than men. I noticed on the way out that the room capacity was marked 120, making me reflect on the upper room scriptural passages from the Acts of the Apostles. I imagined experiencing the emotions felt by those gathered in the upper room.

On my drive home, I reflected on why the Blessed Virgin asks us to celebrate the First Saturday Devotions. She "revealed" to me that devotions are for our benefit, but we are like bouquets of roses, adorning her Son's altar. It was an uplifting devotional experience for me today: first praying the rosary in communion with the daily rosary group, and secondly, enjoying Holy Mass celebrated by a vividly joyful priest. I visited the Blessed Sacrament Chapel afterward and meditated on the Luminous Mysteries in company with Our Blessed Mother.

Sunday, January 6, 2013 – The Epiphany of the Lord

I enjoyed the homilies of three priests today. First from the televised Mass at 5:30 a.m. from the San Francisco diocese, then on the Internet from the Mayo Clinic in Minnesota, and finally the 11:00 a.m. Mass at my home parish, Saint Peter's. I very much enjoy Father Larry Gillick's Sunday reflections on the Creighton University Daily Prayer website.

My prayers today are offered for my cousin Irene, her husband Richard, and their daughter Samantha, that they will reconcile with my Uncle Nick. Uncle Nick and his daughter Irene haven't spoken to each other for over two years and Uncle is ninety-three years old today.

I felt very close to the Lord today and to Our Blessed Mother in several quiet moments of prayer. My best success today was avoiding my habitual sin of overeating. God willing, I will continue in His grace and begin to have a better attitude toward eating.

I'm reading a book entitled *Rediscover Catholicism*. It's saying a lot overall about spirituality. There was a wonderful story about the Holy Eucharistic, about a tiny monstrance, hidden in a ruined wall in oppressed modern-day China. A priest, visiting China incognito, followed a community of Chinese Christians risking their lives to traverse into the woods for a group adoration of the Blessed Sacrament. The consecrated Host had been hidden in the monstrance for ten years. It made me ashamed that the Blessed Sacrament is only a two-minute drive from my house, and that there are over one hundred other adoration chapels throughout my diocese, all totally and safely accessible. My own heart, however, doesn't come close to the zeal of those Chinese faithful.

A Conclave to Elect a New Pope

Friday, March 1, 2013 – First Friday Devotions

I enjoyed my First Friday Devotions and the first day of my novena to the Holy Spirit. I moved my books and study materials to the kitchen table in hopes of watching less television. I fear it's resulted in my eating too much with the nearness of food in the kitchen. This is a pitiful rationalization for my sins of gluttony.

I'm keeping watch over the conclave developments and becoming excited about the election of our new Pope. I'm happy for Holy Father Pope Benedict in his well-earned retirement. He must have had a marvelous first day at Castel Gandolfo.

So far I've fulfilled my First Friday and First Saturday devotions for the Year of Faith. I've learned much from the various prayer books and Internet sites I've been visiting. There's an EWTN daily report from the Vatican on the conclave and other developments. I'm very fortunate to have all these resources at my fingertips.

Saturday, March 2, 2013 – Second Week of Lent

(First Saturday Devotions – Divine Motherhood)

I enjoyed and completed all First Saturday Devotion prayers and actions today. I went to Holy Spirit Parish in Fairfield for a face-to-face confession. It had been three weeks since my last visit and I felt very much depleted of God's grace.

The gospel reading today on the Prodigal Son is one of my favorites. It continues to reveal God's patient and inexhaustible love for us. My thoughts today enabled me to see that we need not be distant from God to be absent from God. We can be right where we are, hidden in our everyday life, and still be isolated from God's grace. Tomorrow will be a special day for Bernadette and me: we'll entertain our Aunt Evangeline on her eighty-first birthday, take a trip to the casino, and go out to lunch.

March 3, 2013 – Third Sunday of Lent

Today was a day of total rest and a day to entertain our Aunt Evangeline. Bernadette and I went to Holy Mass at 11:00 a.m. and I drove to Stockton to pick up Auntie.

I always enjoy praying the rosary while driving and had plenty of time to pray a Sorrowful Rosary for penance.

It was a long visit with family today, but very enjoyable. My sister Jackie and brother Mike came over and with Auntie Van here, we had a lively visit. The food was much too much.

While Steve and Auntie Van watched movies, I fell asleep on the couch. I got a phone call from my son Calvin and his girlfriend at 10:30 p.m., telling me they were stranded with their bicycles at the Davis Train Station. There had been a train incident where a man was killed. The subsequent delays left them waiting for a train that would never come. I picked them up and drove them back to Sacramento. I had just enough time to pray my novena to the Holy Spirit at 11:15 p.m. when I returned home.

Monday, March 4, 2013 – Third Week of Lent

(Saint Casimir)

The readings for today's liturgy are relating the idea that God works miracles through ordinary things. In the case of Naaman, a military commander, the waters of the Jordan cured his leprosy. Actually, the waters had little to do with it. It was Naaman's conversion of attitude. The same simplicity exists when we receive the miracle of absolution through the Sacrament of Reconciliation. It's a simple ordinary formula: tell your sins to the priest and he absolves you through the power of Christ and in His name. Once again, in still another simple and ordinary form, the Body and Blood, Soul and Divinity of our Lord are present in the Holy Bread of the Altar. What is simpler than bread and the few words "This is My Body"? All are simply astounding miracles in the simplest form!

I had a very nice spiritual day and a good time taking Auntie Vangie to lunch and a casino trip celebrating her eighty-first birthday.

Tuesday, March 5, 2013 – Third Week of Lent

This day was mostly devoted to a continuing visit with Auntie Vangie. It's the last day of her three-day stay and she's enjoying our company very much. In between visiting with Bernadette and my Aunt, I interspersed prayers and meditations. Our son Steve was very thoughtful and rented several movies for us to watch throughout this visit.

As I was driving Auntie home, I became absorbed in our conversation, and missed the turnoff to Stockton. I drove for over thirty minutes before realizing I was heading to Reno. This allowed for an extended visit. When we reached Auntie's apartment, my cousin John-John was there to greet us. We all had another nice visit. It was 11:30 p.m. when I got back home. I enjoyed washing dishes and cleaning the kitchen before going to bed.

Wednesday, March 6, 2013 – Third Week of Lent

I very much enjoyed the company of the base hospital chapel community at daily Mass today. Father Greg had his usual fine homily, and Fred, the "old-school" organist, was there to play my favorite songs.

There were thirty people at Mass, including the faithful regulars. I had a chance to read the Catechism when I arrived about an hour early, and after Mass I visited the tiny Blessed Sacrament room to pray a Joyful Rosary for John and Beverly, my dear friends in Florida.

Earlier I experienced a productive morning prayer session. The Creighton University Lenten Prayer site was particularly joyful and pleasing to visit.

Thursday, March 7, 2013 – Third Week of Lent

(Saints Perpetua and Felicity)

I over-did my study for the upcoming conclave and the activities leading up to the election of our next pope. Subsequently I'm drained of all energy and unable to sleep well. However, I feel well informed about the historic events unfolding around me.

My prayers today were very robotic and dry. But I did complete all the elements of my Holy Spirit novena, rosary, and morning prayers. I listened to the congregation of cardinals at their Solemn Vespers, as they venerated the Blessed Sacrament at Saint Peter's Basilica.

Friday, March 8, 2013 – Third Week of Lent

(Saint John of God)

I was especially moved by the homily presented at the televised daily Mass from Toronto. It cited the holiness and loving forgiveness of Hosea as he continued to love his wife unconditionally, even after she repeatedly engaged in adultery.

Today, as well as the day before, I felt very tired and empty of all energy. My prayer sessions were robotic and I needed to take naps frequently throughout the day.

I was very good about keeping up-to-date on the happenings of the coming conclave. The main source of information has been the EWTN channel.

I guess I've been ignoring my wife and son these past few days in favor of keeping my conclave watch. I'll try to rectify that today.

I spent some time in the evening preparing a few more frozen meals for Uncle Nick. I hope to visit him tomorrow. Bernadette is making his favorite fried catfish nuggets this evening.

It was my first time to read about the life of Saint John of God today. I was so amazed and humbled by this wonderful saint.

SATURDAY, MARCH 9, 2013 – THIRD WEEK OF LENT

(Saint Frances of Rome)

This day was dedicated to visiting Uncle Nick, taking him shopping, and driving him around on various errands. This took about five hours from 9:00 a.m. to 2:00 p.m. I took advantage of the drive to and from Uncle Nick's to say my prayers. Some of my most satisfying prayers, as a matter of fact, take place while I'm driving.

I finished my novena to the Holy Spirit today. The prayers were not the best in the world, but it was a new experience praying to the Holy Spirit at all. With the upcoming conclave, this mode of prayer is very appropriate.

I prayed for success regarding my son Steve's film shoot of a scene from the movie *A Few Good Men*. When I saw Steve this evening, he said that the project went very well. We enjoyed watching and discussing the film again tonight. It's funny; we've seen the movie several times, but still find things we hadn't noticed almost every time we sit through it once more.

I just remembered to look up Saint Frances of Rome on YouTube.

Sunday, March 10, 2013 – Fourth Sunday of Lent

We got a phone call from Sarah and Anthony early this morning saying that they'd be coming over to do laundry.

Not feeling like entertaining our children all day long, we "escaped" to the city of Winters for Sunday Mass and a trip to the casino for lunch. We left forty dollars and a note on the kitchen table wishing Sarah and Anthony well.

Father Mike Hebda gave a beautiful homily on the gospel reading of the Prodigal Son. As old and as familiar as this reading is, Father managed to say many new things about the story. One of the key thoughts he brought up is that, like the older son, we often refuse to embrace those who repent.

Monday, March 11, 2013 – Fourth Week of Lent

(Week of the Conclave)

I relocated my reading materials to the kitchen table and concentrated on prayers for the upcoming conclave.

I submitted my name for the German student-initiated program called "Adopt a Cardinal." The group randomly gives you a cardinal's name and you are asked to pray for him throughout the conclave. I received the name of Cardinal Stanislaw Ryiko of Poland. He is the organizer of World Youth Day and the head of the Pontificate of the Laity.

I completed my usual daily prayer routines. There was no special inspiration or feelings of great satisfaction. I think I enjoyed my short time of prayer out in the sunshine, especially the music of the birds and the feel of the warm sun.

Tuesday, March 12, 2013 – Conclave Day #1

Day One of the conclave was uneventful. The procession into the Sistine Chapel was a magnificent thing to witness. Seeing the events unfold on television actually might have advantages over being there in person. I had an erratic eating and sleeping day trying to keep up-to-the-minute with the conclave.

It keeps occurring to me that when leaders were chosen in Sacred Scripture, the most unlikely candidate was always chosen. For example, David was chosen; and Joseph was selected over his eleven brothers. This is why I still have intuitions that the Archbishop Tagle of Manila may be chosen as our new pope.

I'll likely preoccupy myself tomorrow focusing primarily on the conclave.

Wednesday, March 13, 2013 – Conclave Day #2

Pope Francis was elected at about noon today. I experienced a wonderful, overwhelming feeling of great joy. I succumbed to evil today, however: as the television was showing the new pope's first address from the balcony above Saint Peter's Square, about thirty seconds into the pope's greeting, my wife Bernadette suddenly changed the TV channel. She couldn't explain what she was looking for. I angrily called out, "What do you think you're doing?" I recovered soon afterward and let Bernadette know that she is far more important than the election of our pope.

I enjoyed several Internet sites on Pope Francis' election and his life story. A Charlie Rose talk show presenting the presidents of two Catholic universities and a prominent author was especially helpful in learning about our new pope.

Thursday, March 14, 2013 – Fourth Week of Lent

I experienced a dry spiritual day, plodding through my Lenten prayers and inattentively watching Holy Father Francis celebrate his first papal Mass. The Holy Father is encouraging us to reflect on the Magnificat of Our Lady which says, "the rich will be sent away empty and the poor shall be exalted." The United States is too rich and the poor are too poor. We must also be poor in spirit like the Holy Father. What a wonderful example of God's grace he's projected in the first days of his pontificate.

It's been nearly two weeks since my last confession and I feel totally drained of God's grace. I must confess and receive reconciliation this Saturday.

Friday, March 15, 2013 – Fourth Week of Lent

Studying the Catechism today, I realized that all of us in the Church have a direct role in purifying the souls of those in Purgatory. Our Mother has asked us to pray for these souls, as we ourselves will be added to the rolls of Purgatory in most likelihood.

We should look at Purgatory as a good thing. It is not condemnation to hell, but a necessary place to purify us enough to enter into God's presence. If not purified, we would surely die at the first sight of God.

This new enlightenment about the blessing of Purgatory does not mean that I will suddenly have the motivation and holy discipline to begin daily prayers for the souls in Purgatory. I'm a prime candidate for Purgatory myself with my laziness and habitual sins. Only God's grace can save me.

I've not felt well the past three days or so. I can probably contribute it to my poor diet and lack of sleep. I've deviated from the model of Jiro the Sushi King who maintains a regular routine. Once you fall off track it's hard getting back on the right path. I will return to healthy eating and good sleep habits in due time.

Saturday, March 16, 2013 – Fourth Sunday of Lent

I was overwhelmed at confession this evening to learn that a single "Hail Mary" is powerful enough to do penance for my many sins. In studying the gospel reading for today's Mass, I realized that we as daily sinners "throw stones" by our refusal to forgive.

Several people I met at Mass today requested prayers. Maria asked me to pray for her daughter's battle with breast cancer, and for a wedding ring she lost. Jim and Louise needed prayers for Jim's upcoming heart surgery, and I noticed a few people around me who were open for prayer: a recent widower, and Gloria, who has neck pains; all need to be lifted up in prayer.

March 17, 2013 – Fifth Sunday of Lent

(Saint Patrick's Day)

I didn't sleep much today, but felt very rested nevertheless. I was up early to complete my prayers before going to Sacramento for a family gathering at my sister Jackie's. There was a wedding for my niece Francesca and her husband Sam yesterday and a lot of family was in town. Everyone was uneasy because Bernadette and I weren't invited to the wedding. My niece and Sam could afford only fifty guests and if Sam couldn't invite some of his aunts and uncles, he had to leave out some of Francesca's aunts and uncles. My sister Jackie stirred the "pot" by insisting that Bernadette and I come anyhow. Good thing we didn't take her advice.

My brother Mike brought me a nice news article from a small New Jersey newspaper on Pope Francis. Mike cooked his delicious Italian chicken with yellow rice and Jackie cooked corned beef and cabbage in honor of Saint Patrick. We were happy to see all the nieces and nephews and my brothers and sister. We came home early enough to watch Pope Francis' Mass at Saint Anne's Parish which is on the Vatican grounds.

Monday, March 18, 2013 – Fifth Week of Lent

(Saint Cyril of Jerusalem)

I reflected today that Saint Joseph was, in a way, the "first pope" of the Church and the head of and protector of the Family of God, which is the Church.

My cousin, Mother Elizabeth of the Trinity, a Carmelite, always headed her correspondence with the letters "JMJ" for the initials of the Holy Family. I've been neglecting my devotion to Saint Joseph, and I hope to correct this from now on.

I'm more and more touched in the heart by the holiness and simplicity of our new Holy Father, Pope Francis. The manner in which he speaks of the Church and of Christ, the Head of our Body, and how he loves Our Blessed Mother, truly invigorates me.

I had a nice visit and conversation with Bernadette this morning about our faith, and how the Lord has abundantly blessed us throughout our lives. How happy we are in God's grace, and how fortunate we are to have His many blessings.

Tuesday, March 19, 2013 – Fifth Week of Lent

(Saint Joseph Novena Day #1)

My prayers today were very brief; I only visited a Saint Joseph Novena Prayer website, and watched a YouTube Sorrowful Rosary video. These prayers were for Jim and Louise. Jim will be going for his artery-clearing operation on April 11. Bernadette and I will drive them to the hospital.

Before the April hospital date, we'll be taking a trip with Jim and Louise to Red Hawk Casino to celebrate their anniversary.

We met a few people from Saint Peter's Parish at the casino today. It was almost like a parish reunion. We also saw our former daughter-in-law, Rhonda. My first son, Calvin, was with Rhonda for about seven years before they broke up. We love Rhonda and are sorry their relationship came to an end. This is very often what takes place when the marriage is not a sacramental marriage fortified by God's grace.

I'm continuing to enjoy very much learning about the day-to-day activities of our Holy Father Pope Francis.

Wednesday, March 20, 2013 – First Day of Spring

(Saint Joseph Novena Day #2)

I had a swollen left foot today, but missed the opportunity to offer my discomforts up to the Lord, and instead complained throughout the day. The novena prayers to Saint Joseph on YouTube are very well done, and the fact that I've ignored devotion to him most of my life is somewhat startling. Saint Joseph actually fills a role model void lacking in my own understanding of Our Blessed Mother and the Lord Himself. I can much more easily identify with attainment of holiness in the example of the man Joseph. He was not immaculately conceived and had no divine nature, but he seemed to perfectly comply with the will of God, especially when he uncompromisingly believed that Jesus was the Christ.

What a lazy and foolish day I allowed myself to have. I watched two movies of not very much consequence except for nostalgic value to me alone. I ate far too many homemade cookies, and over-indulged in barbecued ribs that Bernadette prepared.

I am happy for my son Steve. He had some shaky experiences leading up to the start of spring break, but everything turned out okay with the help of Bernadette's prayers.

Thursday, March 21, 2013

(Saint Joseph Novena Day #3)

I watched a movie called *Courageous* that was about living and sharing the faith. The movie was quite the good tonic for keeping in mind why I exist. I again did some reckless eating throughout the day. This habitual sin has two obvious evils. First, it shows a lack of care for my personal health and well-being; and secondly it's a clear misuse of God's gifts. God's grace alone can save me.

I sent an email to my brothers and sisters today sharing the faith. I realize that they grow weary of hearing about the Lord and His presence in our lives, but as Pope Francis has clearly professed, we must all proclaim the Good News.

My son Steve is on a two-week spring break. I must be more considerate to him in regards to my frequent spiritual activities. He's often commented that being in our house is like being in church. There's always spiritual music playing or various homilies or religious programs "blasting," he says, from the computer or television. I mentioned that I'd try to wear earphones.

Friday, March 22, 2013

(Saint Joseph Novena Day #4)

A very uneventful day, both in a worldly and spiritual sense. I completed day number four of my Saint Joseph novena for Jim and Louise, and visited the Lenten Prayer site. I watched the daily Mass from Saint Michael's College in Toronto. The celebrant offered the Mass for his mother who had passed into eternal life in 2011. The televised Mass was made possible by a donation from his father.

I listened to Pope Francis give an address to the Diplomatic Corps. All of his homilies and addresses have been wonderful yet simple. I'm happy that the pope is in the news every day and I hope the "novelty" doesn't wear out too soon.

I'm enjoying spring break visits with my son Steve. We watched the Arnold Palmer Golf Tournament together and a movie, *The Hobbit*.

Saturday, March 23, 2013 - Saint Turibius of Mogrovejo

(Saint Joseph Novena Day #5)

I made sure to wake up very early this morning to do my prayers, especially the novena to Saint Joseph, for Jim and Louise.

Most of my day was spent in a five-hour visit with Uncle Nick. I brought him seven most-appreciated, home-cooked frozen meals. I drove him around the town of Isleton. We visited the museum, an art gallery, and a local ice cream shop where Uncle bought some bread, while we visited with several of his friends. Our last stop was the grocery store. By the time we returned to Uncle's house, both of us were worn out. It's been my habit to visit Uncle about twice a month lately. I hope to continue these visits for some time.

Actually, I was awake at 4:00 a.m. earlier in the day, and had plenty of time to do dishes and clean the kitchen, cook breakfast, and take a leisurely shower.

When I returned home from Uncle Nick's, I had a nice visit with my son Steve as we watched a re-broadcast of the Arnold Palmer Golf Tournament.

March 24, 2013 – Palm Sunday

I felt especially full of the Holy Spirit, both during morning prayers and at the Palm Sunday Mass at Saint Peter's. I listened to the Holy Father's homily before attending Mass, and was overjoyed to hear him make "three" points in his presentation.

He stressed three words: "Joy," "Cross," and "Youth." The great number of youth present at Saint Peter's Square loudly cheered when he spoke of the upcoming World Youth Day, to be held this June in Buenos Aires. One thing Pope Francis said, regarding Youth Day, is that no matter how old we are, we are forever young at heart because of Jesus Our Lord.

Father Eduardo celebrated Mass at Saint Peter's today and was assisted by Deacon John King. Father's very short homily was very exciting. He asked everyone to question who they most closely resembled in the narrative of Christ's passion. I'm afraid that I'm very often one of the crowd who calls out, "Crucify Him."

I began planning for a celebration of my mother's fifth anniversary of passing into eternal life. We're hoping to host a rosary, lunch, and Bingo party on June 9.

Monday, March 25, 2013 - Holy Week

We had a visit from our dear friend "Home" Huerta who often spends an afternoon when she returns from hospital appointments. We ended up going on a trip to the casino. Bernadette and "Home," especially, had fun. Jim and Louise were celebrating the week of their wedding anniversary. We'll be joining them for dinner and a trip to Red Hawk Indian Casino on Wednesday.

I've thoroughly enjoyed the Lenten season, which was made all the more special by Pope Emeritus Benedict XVI's earlier Year of Faith proclamation, and of course, the election of Pope Francis. It's such a blessing to have continuing media coverage of the Holy Father.

Being a long-time golf enthusiast, I was happy to see Tiger Woods return to recognized status as the world's number-one golfer. I so much enjoyed watching the Arnold Palmer Invitational Tournament this week. Tiger won for the eighth time to match Sam Sneed.

Tuesday, March 26, 2013 - Holy Week

The Creighton University Daily Reflection was by Father Roc, one of the Saint Louis Jesuit musicians I visit almost daily on YouTube. I've been taking them and their music totally for granted. I finally got around to sending Father Roc a "thank you" message by email. Today, I had a nice email exchange with my brother Mike, who lives in New Jersey.

I've written a multiple-choice test on my mother's life as part of our gathering this upcoming June 9. The twenty-five question test is loaded with trivia and commonly known facts within our family about "Grandma Jean." There will be a mystery prize (a Yatzee game) for whoever scores the highest mark. I had my brother Mike take the test today and he scored 23 out of 25. When the celebration day comes, however, not all of us children of Grandma Jean will be eligible for the prize.

Wednesday, March 27, 2013 - Holy Week

(Jim and Louise's Anniversary)

I had an acceptable day of prayer. Besides visiting my usual Creighton University and Toronto Daily Mass Internet sites, I got caught up on my *Magnificat* Year of Faith daily reflection book. I'm also up-to-date on the daily Mass *Magnificat* missal.

Today was Jim and Louise's forty-sixth wedding anniversary, and Bernadette and I went on a trip with them to Red Hawk Indian Casino. Jim won a ten thousand dollar jackpot, so the casino gave him a free two hundred dollar meal ticket. We all went for a free steakhouse treat. Bernadette also hit a jackpot of three hundred dollars, which enabled me to bring home a hundred dollars to give Steve for his spring break fun. He doesn't get paid until next Monday and is a poor college student.

Now I prepare for the great Triduum. I look forward to watching all the events celebrated by the Holy Father on EWTN. It will be a magnificent event tomorrow when he washes the feet of juvenile detention inmates.

March 28, 2013 – Holy Thursday

The highlight of my spiritual day was to visit the Blessed Sacrament and pray the Luminous Rosary in the company of Our Blessed Mother. Father Eduardo was there making preparations for the evening Mass. Clare was also there, with two other women, rehearsing the Stations of the Cross.

After my visit, I went shopping for birthday cards for my sisters Debby and Jonie. I found two very nice cards at the dollar store, paying only one dollar for two. I had five dollars left over to buy a box of M&M candies and Milk Duds for Steve.

I had a very difficult time getting to sleep this evening, so just stayed awake visiting with Steve and listening to Oldies music. I took a drive to the post office to mail some birthday cards, and cooked and packed some frozen meals for Uncle Nick.

I watched videos of Pope Francis washing the feet of the juvenile inmates. It was especially dear to my heart because I was a juvenile hall counselor for fifteen years as my second career. I printed a photo of His Holiness washing and kissing the feet of one of the inmates, and added it to my papal photo gallery in our kitchen.

March 29, 2013 – Good Friday

I absorbed myself in prayer and meditation on this Good Friday. The homily at the Vatican celebration of the Lord's passion, by a humble Franciscan priest, was superb. I found great solace in the little *Magnificat* Mass booklet, and was similarly delighted by the Creighton University Lenten Prayer site. The Toronto Television Broadcast of the passion readings accompanied by a series of short homilies seemed far superior to the Saint Peter's Basilica rendition of the readings.

I enjoyed praying with help from several YouTube videos, including a Holy Land version of the Sorrowful Rosary, a Stations of the Cross video called "The Incredible Stations of the Cross," and several news articles on Pope Francis.

Although I failed miserably at observing a devoted fasting and abstinence regimen throughout the whole of Lent, I had a few shining moments observing the Saint Anthony Abbot "sundown fast." I was generally satisfied with the rest of my Lenten observances in this holy Year of Faith.

March 30, 2013 - Holy Saturday

It was kind of a mediocre day for me in regards to prayer, but I had time to rest. I enjoyed doing simple little tasks around the house and had plenty of time to reflect on all my many blessings. I also had time to reflect on how well I've been doing physically and spiritually.

The last day of the year's first quarter is about to end, and if I graded myself I would receive a "C minus," both physically and spiritually. I'm determined to do much better in the second quarter of this Year of Faith.

One of the successful things I did in January was to follow the philosophy of the famous sushi chef, Jiro. It would be good to practice doing the same things day to day. My habitual sin of poor eating habits triumphed over me this first quarter. I remember being more successful when I wrote down the meals I planned to eat the night before. I'll return to this method for April and see how it goes. I'm very happy in God's grace with the progress I'm making in prayer.

March 31, 2013 - Easter Sunday

I received an early morning wake-up call from John Kovach today, so I decided to attend 8:00 a.m. Mass at Saint Peter's. It was totally crowded, with standing room only, but I arrived early enough to go to confession and find a good seat. I sat next to Joe Chacon.

Father Eduardo presided and Deacon John King assisted. I felt relieved to have the Lenten season come to a conclusion, but a little empty knowing that I'd have to engineer my own prayer routine for April. Never fear, I've already found a nice novena to the Sacred Heart of Jesus.

I was able to complete my goal of one hundred pages per month of Catechism study this evening. The sections on the liturgy were a bit tedious, but the next hundred pages on the seven sacraments should be more enjoyable.

This writing concludes my journal for the first quarter of the Year of Faith. What a wonderful time it's been with the election of Pope Francis. I'm savoring the constant news coverage and messages to come, while knowing that after the Easter season, it may very well decrease in frequency.

Fast-Forward to Present Day

(Final Remarks by Me, Zacchaeus)

Francesco needn't have concerned himself that the newsworthiness of Pope Francis would dwindle. It is three years into his pontificate and he still prevails as a constant presence in world-wide media attention. No world leader or popular rock star today could ever draw crowds numbering in the millions as Pope Francis does. The Holy Father will come to Philadelphia in September of 2015 for the World Meeting of Families. Francesco will be glued to the EWTN coverage while he makes final preparations to celebrate the Year of Mercy.

Pope Francis Homily: Mass at Casa Santa Marta, January 10, 2015

"This is the doctrine of two commandments: the most important is 'You shall love the Lord, your God, with all your heart, with all your soul, and with all your mind. This is the greatest and the first commandment. The second is like it: You shall love your neighbor as yourself.' To get to the first we must ascend the steps of the second: that means that through our love for our neighbor we can get to know God, who is love. Only through loving can we reach love."

Pope Francis: Friday, March 13, 2015 St Peter's Basilica

"Dear brothers and sisters, I have often thought of how the Church may render more clear her mission to be a witness to mercy; and we have to make this journey. It is a journey that begins with spiritual conversion. Therefore, I have decided to announce an **Extraordinary Jubilee** that has at its center the mercy of God. It will be a **Holy Year of Mercy**. We want to live in the light of the word of the Lord: 'Be merciful, even as your Father is merciful' (cf. Luke 6:36). And this especially applies to confessors! So much mercy!

"This Holy Year will commence on the next Solemnity of the Immaculate Conception: December 8, 2015, and will conclude on Sunday, November 20, 2016, the Solemnity of Our Lord Jesus Christ, King of the Universe and living face of the Father's mercy.

"I entrust the organization of this Jubilee to the Pontifical Council for Promoting the New Evangelization, in order that it may come to life as a new step on the Church's journey in her mission to bring the gospel of mercy to each person.

"I am confident that the whole Church, which is in such need of mercy for we are sinners, will be able to find in this Jubilee the joy of rediscovering and rendering fruitful God's mercy, with which we are all called to give comfort to every man and every woman of our time. Do not forget that God *forgives all*, and God *forgives always*. Let us never tire of asking forgiveness. Let us henceforth entrust this year to the Mother of Mercy, that she turn her gaze upon us and watch over our journey: our penitential journey, our year-long journey with an open heart, to receive the indulgence of God, to receive the mercy of God."

*Mother, I am yours now and forever.
Through you and with you
I always want to belong
completely to Jesus...*

~ Francesco

REFERENCES

PART I

Page 15: "You are Mine lyrics," Yahoo online video search

Page 15: "Psalm 139," Online USCCB Books of the Bible

Page 18-19: "1 Corinthians Chapter 13," Online USCCB Books of the Bible

Page 20-21: "The ACTS Prayer Model," truereflectionsinchrist.com

Page 21: "Saint Francis de Sales," Online Introduction to the Devout Life

Page 23: "Lectio Divina," gvdays.org/lectiodivina

PART II

Page 32: "Suspice of Saint Ignatius of Loyola," loyolapress.com

Page 34: "The Corporal Works of Mercy" and "The Spiritual Works of Mercy," catholicculture.org

Page 37: Frank Padilla - frankpadilla.com

Part III

Page 50-54: "Way of Total Consecration," fisheaters.com

Page 55: "Holy Voluntary Slavery," ssvmusa.org/marianvow

Page 56: "Letter to Philomen," Online, USCCB Books of the Bible

Page 77: "Franciscan Friars Homilies Online," Online Yahoo videos

Page 79-80: "After Consecration," fisheaters.com

Page 82: "Mary the Mother of God," catholic.com/tracts/mary-mother-of-god

Page 83: "The Blessed Virgin Mary," catholic.com/tracts/mary-ever-virgin

Page 84: "Mary Queen of Peace," en.wikipedia.org/wiki/Our_Lady_of_Peace

Page 85: "Mary Queen of all Saints," ainglkiss.com/saints/queen.htm

Page 85-86: "Our Lady of the Miraculous Medal," olrl.org/lives/laboure.shtml

Page 86-87: "Our Lady of Perpetual Help," cmri.org

Page 87-88: "Our Lady of Mount Carmel," motherofallpeoples.com

Page 88-89: "Our Lady of the Snows," roman-catholic-saints.com

Page 89: "Our Lady of Sorrows," roman-catholic-saints.com

Page 89-90: "The Seven Sorrows," angelfire.com/md3/fel/test.html

Page 90: "Our Lady of Knock," roman-catholic-saints.com

Page 91: "Our Lady of Guadalupe," roman-catholic-saints.com

Page 92: "Our Lady of Lourdes," roman-catholic-saints.com

Page 93: "Our Lady of Fatima," roman-catholic-saints.com

Page 95-97: "The History of the Rosary," ewtn.com/library/ANSWERS

Page 125: "Pope Francis Homily, January 10, 2015," Online Yahoo Videos

Page 126: "Pope Francis Homily, March 13, 2015," Online Yahoo Videos

The author pledges all profits from this little book to the Sisters of Mercy and the Loaves and Fishes organization in Sacramento, California.

About Sister Libby and the Loaves and Fishes Organization

What a remarkable journey I have been privileged to walk in mercy! After serving seven years in the United States Air Force and receiving my Masters in social work, I entered the Sisters of Mercy on September 2, 1990. Back then, we were a small community of one hundred sisters from Auburn, California. Today, we are an institute active across the Americas and are over three thousand strong!

I embraced my call from God to serve our "poor, sick, and uneducated," and chose the motto "Pan de Vida": Bread of Life. God's mysterious direction led me to only two ministries in my twenty-five years of service: six years with Mercy Housing, and the rest where I continue to serve as executive director of the Sacramento Loaves & Fishes, by which I am blessed and honored to "feed the hungry and shelter the homeless" on a daily basis. Truly, the "works of mercy" are alive through me because of all those who have walked with me on this journey: my sisters, associates, and family.

Sister Libby Fernandez, RSM
Sister of Mercy, Silver Jubilee 2015

 **About Leonine Publishers**

Leonine Publishers LLC makes fine Catholic literature available to Catholics throughout the English-speaking world. Leonine Publishers offers an innovative "hybrid" approach to book publication that helps authors as well as readers. Please visit our web site at www.leoninepublishers.com to learn more about us. Browse our online bookstore to find more solid Catholic titles to uplift, challenge, and inspire.

Our patron and namesake is Pope Leo XIII, a prudent, yet uncompromising pope during the stormy years at the close of the 19th century. Please join us as we ask his intercession for our family of readers and authors.

Do you have a book inside you? Visit our web site today. Leonine Publishers accepts manuscripts from Catholic authors like you. If your book is selected for publication, you will have an active part in the production process. This book is an example of our growing selection of literature for the busy Catholic reader of the 21st century.

www.leoninepublishers.com

www.ingramcontent.com/pod-product-compliance
Lightning Source LLC
Chambersburg PA
CBHW031358040426
42444CB00005B/342